Tithing for Catholics

From the Poustinia, Volume 1

Derek Williams

Published by Derek Williams, 2019.

To the Lord Jesus Christ, the greatest and only evangelist in the Church which he established.May he who began this work bring it to completion in the hearts of the readers.

Philippians 1:6

TITHING

FOR

CATHOLICS

THE DEPOSIT THAT GUARANTEES THE BLESSING.

DEREK WILLIAMS

* * * * *

Copyright ©Derek Williams 2019

DEREK WILLIAMS

* * * * *

Published by: *Verbum Publications*

First published 2019

"Test me in this" says the Lord (Malachi 3:10).

* * * * *

ACKNOWLEDGEMENTS

First, I have to thank my wife Lynn, and my children, Catherine (Cat), Michael, Hannah, Samuel, Joshua and Sarah. Without their support, encouragement, prayers and putting up with my tantrums, not a lot would happen.

Throughout this volume I have quoted many extracts. These have been very gratefully taken from *www.blueletterbible.org/*[1] and are the NASB translation.

Cover: background image created by jcomp: *https://www.freepik.com/ free-photos-vectors/background*

My thanks to Charles Whitehead for inviting me to write this book several years ago.

It has taken a while to get it into print.

Thank you to Nick Clovis whose artistic genius designed the cover.

---

1. *http://www.blueletterbible.org/*

He will always give the glory to God.

Thank you to Fr Luke Goymour for checking my theology and putting in plenty of suggested amendments. Thanks also to Tom Goymour of Verbum Publications who has done the edit to this book. Both have given me loads of encouragement – very gratefully received.

I give thanks to God. Although I wrote this book, I definitely would not have done it without his help. Virtually every sentence was prayed into being.

Finally, thanks goes to Mary, the Queen of peace. Were it not for her maternal presence in my life I think would definitely have lost the plot a long time ago.

DISCLAIMER

I am not telling you to tithe, I am not even recommending it, I am just placing before you what I understand to be the teaching from God's Word on the topic and the possible fruit that can come from tithing. I am also trying to direct your heart to the Kingdom of God so that you can experience a new liberty in your finances (or 'from' your finances).

If you choose to tithe as a result of reading this book that is entirely your own free choice. I will not be held responsible for how yyou spend your own money, but be assured, I have prayed for the floodgates to be opened wide for everybody who reads this book.

God bless you – abundantly.

Introduction

A letter from the author

Dear Friend,

This book may well challenge the life into you. What I have written is not intended to make any suggestion of an obligatory practice, but it is to assist you in 'going the extra mile' (cf. Mt 5:41).

All of the books I have ever read on the topic of tithing, and all the talks I have listened to have focussed almost exclusively on money. For example, if you sow into 'x ministry' you will reap 'x money' in return. My approach in this book is to teach you what God has given you, what he is offering to you every day, and what he has stored up for you in eternity. The tithe you give to God is a response to the immeasurable gift he has for you. Now this needs to be understood at the outset; A a tithe is a measure of a financial freewill gift that you are giving to God through Church or some Christian charity. You 'measure' the gift, usually at ten percent of your income. On the other hand, God's gift to us is 'without measure' and the scriptures testify to this frequently.

God's gift to us is without measure; our gift to him is measured!

The more we measure our gift to God (the more we give via Church/ charity), the more we are free to fully receive what he is offering to us. As finite creatures our gift is always going to be very limited. As an infinite God his gift to us is always without limit. The only limits are based on what we tend to hold back. The more we can give, the more we can receive! That is a very simple matter worth repeating in case you missed it:

The more we give; the more we will receive.

In order to get the fullness of what God wants to communicate through this book, please consider the following:

1. A prayer to the Holy Spirit. He is the Spirit of freedom (2 Cor. 3:17) and only when a person has experienced a certain freedom can they freely give more to the Lord. When a person gives in this way, they are free to receive more from God, *'a full measure, pressed down and flowing over'*

(cf. Luke. 6:38).

This is the famous prayer to the Holy Spirit written by Cardinal Mercier. Please follow the instructions – it will make a big difference:

' I am going to reveal to you the secret of sanctity and happiness. Every day for five minutes control your imagination and close your eyes to all the noises of the world in order to enter into yourself. Then, in the sanctuary of your baptised soul (which is the temple of the Holy Spirit) speak to that Divine Spirit, saying to Him:

O Holy Spirit, beloved of my soul, I adore You. Enlighten me, guide me, strengthen me, console me. Tell me what I should do; give me Your orders. I promise to submit myself to all that You desire of me and to accept all that You permit to happen to me. Let me only know Your Will.

If you do this, your life will flow along happily, serenely, and full of consolation, even in the midst of trials. Grace will be proportioned to the trial, giving you the strength to carry it and you will arrive at the Gate of Paradise, laden with merit. This submission to the Holy Spirit is the secret of sanctity.'

Cardinal Mercier

2. Jesus is the Teacher. St John Paul II once proclaimed that 'Jesus is the only one who teaches with authority.' Although I have typed the

words in this book, it has been done through many hours of prayers and pondering God's Word – many, many hours. I believe that Jesus has taught me, and I have tried to write as the teaching has flowed through my heart. I invite you to ask Jesus to teach you. Ask him to be your teacher. That way not only will you quite possibly enjoy what is written, but it will flow through your heart and liberate you to live the message, which will require courage.

3. Nobody can afford to tithe. Tithing requires freedom. Not freedom from financial restraint, this is impossible. Freedom from the fears, worries and anxieties that tend to dominate the fallen human condition. Only when a person is living the life of grace are they free to live according to the Word of God, and then they are liberated to give themselves more fully into God's Kingdom.

4. The purpose of tithing is to give in to the Kingdom of God so that the world can be evangelized. This is the main purpose of the Church's existence. There are many other charitable activities which are fantastic and important, (for example, the author sometimes gives part of his tithe to Mary's Meals), but our number one area for investment needs to become the furtherance of God's Kingdom on earth because this is the most important.

Why do some tithe and others don't?

I don't think there is a straightforward answer to this question, but like many other 'faith' questions it can be answered broadly with the following suggestions:

1. When a person has had an encounter with Christ and they have been filled with the Holy Spirit, there comes a certain liberation to their hearts. They want to *give,* and do so generously. Everybody I know who has had this encounter wants to give more.

2. For most people their hard-earned wages remain their own. For a person who has had the above encounter, their wages are seen as a gift from God and they want to give him something back, they want to be generous to God. It is relationship based.

3. Tithing is not to do with the purse, but the heart. If the money has the person then no tithing is possible. If the person has the money they are free in their relationship with God and will freely give more to the Body of Christ.

4. When a Christian who tithes or has been filled with the Spirit gives money to the Church or a Church-based charity (evangelical organisation, pro-life, etc.), they tend to do so because they see it as giving their money back to God. It is not seen as necessarily going to the charity, per se, but being returned to God. This is fundamentally important. I give my tithe into the building up of the Kingdom of God on earth, not to an earthly institution!

So, we begin the journey of discovering what tithing is with these simple principles in place. A reminder:

1. Pray to the Holy Spirit before every chapter.

2. Jesus is your teacher

3. Tithing is not about giving to a charitable organisation but about returning a nominal tenth of your income to God, who leaves you with 90%.

4. If we want to see our churches growing again we need to review our financial giving. The fundamental purpose of tithing and that of the existence of the Church is to enable ... to *harvest* the evangelisation of the world.

Finally, in the Bible there does not appear to be a fundamental distinction between tithing and first fruits. I am sure there is a difference but for the purposes of this book I am going to treat them as somewhat indistinct. I ask the reader not to be scrupulous in finding fault but to join me in the journey and enjoy the ride.

Why a tenth (10%)?

The idea is that 10% must be set apart and given to the Lord, via the priest. My understanding is that in Jewish Law, 10 men can form a synagogue. If each of the 10 fulfils his vow, then the priest has enough to live on as well.

(Ref: Christianity.stackexchange.com.)

I was initially going to pack this book with testimonies of financial miracles, how people overcame financial problems through regular tithing. However, I started reading Charles Whitehead's book, *Towards a fuller Life in the Holy Spirit* and found the following quote, 'I've taken a decision to rely on the Scriptures to challenge any sceptics. After all:

'The word of god is living and active...'

Hebrews 4:12.

I've learned that God can speak for himself – we don't have to defend him, only proclaim him. Thus this book will be centred on God's Word with possibly the occasional testimony.

* * * * *

1. A Personal Testimony

In 1989 I was virtually lapsed from my faith, attending Sunday Mass but not really being present. My mind was darkened to divine revelation and I was dead in my sin:

'They are darkened in their understanding and separated from the life of God because of the ignorance that is in them due to the hardening of their hearts.'

Ephesians 4:18

I received communion occasionally because Mass was the occasion on which one could! However, I had not been to confession for some years, possibly since my mid-teens, though I don't really remember. My personal prayer life was an occasional 'God, please help me' but more of a despairing cry for help than a faith-filled expectation that God would intervene. Nonetheless, I called myself a catholic! It was a bit like calling myself an athlete because I walked the dog! In other words, and I say this in hindsight, I was somewhat fake with my faith; going to church and telling people I was catholic, but not living the faith.

The idea of giving money to the church was as far removed from me as that of climbing Mount Everest – I am scared of heights! My argument was why should I give money to an apparently wealthy institution that does not do anything for me.

In Feb 1990 all of this changed. I made my first confession in many years in Sept 1989 because I was going to Ireland, the place where the terrorists of the time came from, the IRA. I was scared enough to run into the confessional. (Note: the trip was absolutely wonderful and I met some very beautiful Irish folks who gave me the warmest welcome you can imagine – as those of you who go to Ireland would testify). After this trip to the confessional things started changing and a priest invited me to attend a prayer meeting in my local parish. After being there for a few weeks the group prayed with me in a very specific way which led to my first personal encounter with God, an encounter that radically changed my life. I gave myself over to a daily personal life of prayer for several hours, I left the serious sin behind and started going to Mass several times a day, and confession once a month. The night that I had this personal encounter I actually gave £1 into the offering, which I thought was being generous.

"It was for freedom that Christ has set us free"

Galatians 5:1

This new found freedom enabled me to give money to the things of God. If we do not have that freedom from sin and grow in our relationship with God, it will not make sense to us that we should give money to His Church. Indeed, why give to something that seemingly does not give you anything in return. Something had to change, and it did!

It is worth noting that at this time I was in debt to the tune of £2000 on an annual salary of approximately £6000. In order to get out of debt things had to change:

- I purchased my first study bible (the NIV study Bible)

- I gave away lots of my personal possessions (books, video's, record collection)

- I sold my car

- I began *spending* several hours a day in personal prayer

- I started attending daily Mass

- I stopped wasting money and started living more frugally

• After doing a short home-based bible study course I started tithing

Note that instead of *spending money,* I began *spending time with God.* All of this was a direct result of being filled with the Holy Spirit.

Within 12 months I had cleared my £2k of debt and was that same amount in credit. After selling my car in 1990, I was given a company car. At Easter 1991 I gave up my well-paid professional job (Field Service Engineer) to join a lay community full-time. I left the community in October 1993 and moved to Peterborough where I met Lynn, my future wife. For over a year I was unemployed, unsure what to do with my life. However, just before we got married, God led me to a job with Barclays. At this point I believe God spoke to my heart, 'you will return to evangelisation when the savings have gone.' My reaction is of course to spend all the savings, but I was sensible enough not to.

Lynn and I brought our first house, with her parents' help in June 1995, shortly after getting back from our honeymoon. 18 months later she gave birth to Catherine (Feb 1997) and we had to live on one salary – still tithing. Indeed, before she left for maternity leave her boss told her 'write to us when you want to return to work'. Lynn had no intention of going back to work because she wanted to be a full-time mother, which is what I wanted for her as well. However, after discussion and prayer we agreed we would take her boss's advice. A few months after Catherine was born Lynn wrote to her boss to say that that she was ready to go back, and he wrote back to her saying the position was redundant and sent her a package which gave us enough money to pay off the balance on the family car. Based purely on this perspective tithing seems to work.

We were then a family of three living on a small salary. In fact I was working for a temp agency! It was a difficult time, but we kept our focus and kept tithing. Ten percent of my income went to a charity on pay day each month.

Shortly after Catherine was born I was given a permanent position, and in 1998 along came Michael Joseph (October 1998). I began studying for work-related qualifications and over the period from my first day of work until about five years into the job I was promoted several times and my salary tripled. I was also being given annual bonuses which amounted to around ten percent of my salary. I was giving ten percent of my salary into the kingdom of God, whilst receiving that back and more besides. It was one of these annual bonuses that enabled us to take the family on pilgrimage to Medjugorje whilst Lynn was expecting our third child, Hannah Mary who was born in January 2003.

In summer 2003 we spent our last savings on double glazing and a conservatory for our house, feeling we could afford it because I was on a good salary. However, I started feeling I was out of place in my workplace and could not shake off this feeling. I felt *called* to '*something*'. Lynn and I went to see my spiritual director, Fr David in Birmingham who told me, 'I was chasing shadows, and that I needed to ask God to make it clear.' I did!

Ten days later I was in the Doctor's surgery as I could not stop shaking. I couldn't even talk to him I was just in tears. The Doctor told me, 'you are going to have a breakdown. Quit work or you will not recover.' God made it clear. I went from the surgery to mass where the gospel reading really spoke to me;

'I am going to prepare a place for you. When it is ready I will come back and take you to where I am."

(cf, John 14:2, 3).

I knew Jesus had everything under control and prepared to tell Lynn the bad (good) news. I resigned from my work in November 2003 with no idea what God wanted from me.

We kept on tithing! We also kept on growing as a family. Lynn conceived Joshua but suffered a miscarriage. She gave birth to Samuel in November 2005, but sadly miscarried Sarah Jane a few years later. However, God has given six beautiful children even if he decided two of them should grow up with him.

Now we skip a few years to May 2016. Sadly, although we kept tithing, we also made a few financial mistakes like buying a house that was big and beautiful, but massively outside our budget leading us into a lot of debt. A huge amount of debt, far too much for us to 'work' through. However, 2016 was a year of Jubilee in many ways.

Shortly after he was elected, Pope Francis announced a Jubilee Year of Mercy running from December 2015 through to the end of November 2016. So what is Jubilee? The word comes from the Hebrew '*Yobel*' and it is a concept that comes straight from the book of Leviticus *(chapter 25)*. Summing it up, this is what Jubilee is about; it begins in the 49th year and runs into the 50th year. It is a bit of a leveller. If a person ran into debt, they were cleared. If a person had to sell their property because of a financial problem, it was restored to them (because the land belongs to God). If a person became a slave, for whatever reason, all slaves were set free. Finally, it was a year of rest for everybody, and for the land. No crops were sown so that the land could rest and recover from the constant farming. Thus:

• All debts are cancelled

• All slaves are set free

• All property is returned to its rightful owner (The Hebrew word for 'returned' is *teshuvah*, which is the equivalent of the Greek *metanoia*, repent)

• Everybody has a year of rest, plus the land rests.

The Jubilee for ancient Israel, begins when the High Priest has taken the blood of a ram into the Holy of Holies, has sprinkled it on the mercy seat which is the top part of the Ark of the Covenant, has come out of the Holy of Holies, picked up the horn of the ram which has been sacrificed (Yobel literally means 'ram's horn') and blown it. When the sound of the ram's horn is heard the above four bullet points come into play. This takes place in early autumn, around late September or early October depending on the Jewish calendar (which is centuries older than ours and was given to them by God).

The amazing aspect about the Pope's call to Jubilee is that four Jubilee's happened at the same time. First there was the Catholic one. Then, we found out that the Jewish Jubilee began in that October. Then, amazingly, and remember, this is essentially the 50th year, Lynn turned 50 in March and I turned 50 in August. Four jubilees. Lynn and I, at the start of it, firmly believed our jubilees were going to result in the above scenario's. Cancellation of debt being a big one, we had a lot of debt.

At the start of the Jubilee year both Lynn and I felt through prayer that it was time to sell our house. As always, we prayed earnestly that God would show us very clearly where he wanted us to move. He did. It was Walsingham. A lovely friend of ours was purchasing a house near Walsingham and invited us to rent it. In May 2016 we sold our house, just after our 21st wedding anniversary, and moved to a little hamlet just outside Walsingham. At midday on the Friday of our move we went to our first Mass at the Catholic National Shrine of Our Lady at Walsingham as 'parishioners'. (The Shrine isn't a parish so there are no parishioners, but it is where I work and we exercise our ministries, as readers, Extraordinary Ministers of Holy Communion, welcomers, etc). It was at the moment as Mass began, indeed, as the midday

Angelus was being said, that the money was transferring and our debts were being cancelled, beginning with our mortgage.

For the purposes of transparency, and to satisfy the curiosity of those who are reading this, plus for the sake of cultivating humility, what exactly were those debts that were cleared? I can't remember the exact figures, but this gives the reader a good idea:

• Mortgage – approximately £240,000 from Northern Rock. This was given to us before the infamous financial crisis after which Norther Rock was nationalised. They gave it to us without necessity for proof of income, so we could virtually borrow whatever we wanted.

• Loan - £10,000

• Credit Card - £10,000. This was moved between two credit card companies each 18 months so that we could have it interest free provided we paid a minimal amount each month.

• Yes - £260,000 of debt. Ouch!

The whole lot was cleared on the sale of our beautiful house, and although we don't own a property anymore, we are debt free and have a little bit of money in the bank. The other great blessing is that we have been able to tithe into our son and daughter's ministries. Both served with NET Ireland and we were able to give them considerable support. Our other daughter has recently signed up to the Ascent Course which is a formation course for young adults involved in Catholic Charismatic Renewal, and we are able to support her.

Throughout this time of running up the debt and clearing it, I was working as a full-time Catholic Lay Evangelist. We lived on Divine Providence. Some may say that God was not giving very well seeing as we had such huge debts. My wife and I would completely disagree: The debts were down to our own greed, our covetousness, and our own sinfulness. God in his faithfulness sustained us completely. We never defaulted at any point, we did not 'lose' our house. I received a good income from the various events I spoke at, the parishes I led seminars at, the conferences for which I was always both amazed and thankful that they would invite me to. Catholics can be remarkably generous when it comes to supporting the work of the evangelist. Plus, we had a small support network who would donate to my ministry every month, and some of them would tithe. Their generosity always amazed and humbled me. They were not just financial donors, Lynn and I always considered them to be our friends.

Ironically, within six months of clearing all of the debt God called me to a sabbatical from evangelisation and I returned to a similar task that I did prior to that work. As I am typing this the truth of the matter has at this very moment dawned on me. For several years I worked as a Portfolio Administrator, that was the official title that I started with when I was in my thirties. I managed investments and eventually became a Portfolio Manager. However, it was an administrative role. After I had moved to Walsingham, although it was to work in evangelisation, it quickly became an administrative role which I am doing to this day. The bitter irony is that I cannot stand administration. It is a heavy cross for me, as those who work with me know - but I am willing.

My sabbatical from evangelisation really began on 25th September 2016, but it has taken me two years to accept it because of my love of parish evangelisation. It has truly been a painful purification as those I work with know very well (I do whine and complain). At the time of writing I am in the process of fully embracing it according to God's Most Holy and Divine Will.

We remain out of debt, we strive to tithe every month (it is a spiritual battle). We try and live in accordance with evangelical poverty, but we do not always manage it very well. However, it is something we lean towards. It frustrates the life out of our children who witness us attempting to live life simpler, then failing miserably. Indeed, it is a standing joke in the household! Thank God that we can laugh about it. The blessing is that we have no problem with giving our money into worthy causes, but we spend time praying and pondering about spending money on other things before we either do – or don't !

I pray that as you, the reader ventures into this book that you will have your eyes opened to giving your hard-earned money into the Kingdom of God and it will change the way you think about the funds you bring into your household. I also pray it will deepen your faith. Indeed, that is my real purpose in writing, that the third person of the Trinity, the Holy Spirit, will open your eyes, open your ears, and fill your heart with peace so that you will be freed up to give yourself more and more into His Kingdom. This is what I beseech God to do, what I beg him to do. If only we were all hungry and thirsty for God's Holy Spirit so that we could grow in our union with Him. This is my heartfelt prayer as you read this book and then continue on your journey of faith.

May it be done to you according to His Word.

(cf, Luke 1:38.)

* * * * *

2. The Deposit that Guarantees the Blessing

'You were sealed with the promised Holy Spirit which is the first instalment of our inheritance toward redemption as God's possession, to the praise of his glory.'

Ephesians 1:13, 14

This chapter is really all about the Holy Spirit. This may sound confusing as you are reading a book on tithing, but when we look closely at the definition of tithing from Genesis 28:22 it will make more sense:

'This stone, which I have set up for a pillar, shall be God's house; and of all that you give me I will surely give one tenth to you.'

Jacob recognises that God gives him 100% and that he is only required, or inspired, to give 10% back to God. In order to comprehend the necessity of returning something to God we must first look at what God has given to us.

Both the Holy Spirit and Jesus are referred to as 'firstfruits' by Saint Paul within a certain context. This is something we will look at in the chapter on firstfruits. In this chapter we will analyse the role of the Holy Spirit as a deposit, given to us by God, which guarantees future blessings. When we consider the great gifts God has given to us, it is likely we will become more generous towards God.

In the quote from Saint Paul's letter to the Ephesians at the beginning of this chapter, the author is telling us that the Holy Spirit is a 'seal' which is the first instalment, that guarantees our inheritance. If we use the biblical language of Saint Paul and apply it to 21st century western culture it gives us the following picture. Imagine you want to buy a brand new car but you have insufficient funds except for a deposit. You find the car of your dreams, and put down a deposit. It is this deposit which guarantees 'blessing'. The blessing is that you have a brand new car which you can treat as if it was yours, in spite of you not having 'paid in full'. You have merely put down a deposit, possibly ten percent. In reality you have probably parted with £1,000 for a vehicle that is worth £10,000, yet you can drive it, insure it, and tax it. It is yours.

If we take this thinking of a 'portion' that enables us to guarantee a blessing, then the Holy Spirit can be understood as the 'deposit', the 'first instalment', the 'guarantee'. What is this blessing that he guarantees? In the analogy just given it is the car that we can drive.

In *Ephesians 1* Saint Paul writes:

'Our inheritance toward redemption as God's possession'.

The Holy Spirit is, in a sense, God's tithe to us. He gives Himself as the Holy Spirit, and that is a guarantee of future blessing. God gives us the tithe that we should give to him! The blessing is the redemption of our bodies. The Holy Spirit already operates within the heart of the believer by sanctifying, convicting us of sin, leading us to encounter Christ, helping us to climb the holy mountain, drawing us to intimacy with God. All of this is a 'portion'. It is not the fullness, but is a sign of that fullness which is to come.

Redemption

The word *redemption* expresses this very well. Imagine you have no money whatsoever but you need food. You have an expensive item of jewellery and take that to the pawnbroker where you exchange it for cash. With the cash you buy the food you need and a lottery ticket. This is the week your numbers come up and you win the multi-million pound jackpot. As the jewellery was a family heirloom you want it back because of its sentimental value. So you go to the pawnbrokers and get the jewellery back using some of your winnings paying the price you were given plus some interest. Thus you have 'redeemed' your jewellery. The act of getting back that which you sold due to hard times is redemption.

Humanity was sold as a slave to sin due to Adam and Eve's actions in the garden of Eden. We were in the spiritual pawn shop and under the slavery of the Devil. When Jesus died on the cross and rose again, he set free those who want freedom. He redeemed them from the power of the Devil. The price paid was the blood of Jesus:

'Realize that you were ransomed (redeemed) from your futile conduct, handed on by your ancestors, not with perishable things like silver or gold, but with the precious blood of Christ as of a spotless, unblemished lamb'

1 Pet 1:18, 19.

When a person has been redeemed by accepting Jesus as Lord and Saviour and receiving baptism, they are filled with the Holy Spirit who is the deposit, guaranteeing eternal blessings. With the outpouring of the Holy Spirit comes peace, joy, love, faithfulness, trust, self control, and other fruits and virtues. However, these are not held to perfection in this life because we only have the deposit, not full ownership! The latter comes in eternity. For now we have to put up with our weaknesses which God uses for the full manifestation of his glorious power (cf. 2 Corinthians 12:9).

However, this becomes the exciting part; because a Christian has been filled with the Holy Spirit, they have been given a grace which guarantees heaven, provided they keep walking on the path of salvation. The Holy Spirit, as it were, brings grace into our lives which works in our hearts towards making us pure and holy so as to inherit the fullness of which he is a portion. When we use this language it is not to diminish the Holy Spirit to a mere 'tenth' of what God is, it is to use human language to explain divine wisdom. We don't get 'ten percent' of the third person of the Trinity; one cannot divide God up into bits. It is really saying that we cannot receive the fullness of God's Spirit in this life because of our sinful nature which does not have the capacity for God in the totality of his infinite glory. The light is too bright for our 'spiritual eyes'. God comes to us in a small way in which we can receive him, like a dimmed light for a person with sensitive eyes. As we receive healing of sin and our souls are transformed, the deposit slowly becomes the fullness (Cf. Ephesians 3:19). The eyes can then handle a brighter light, a bit like when a person wakes up in the morning and needs a gentle light at first because their eyes have been used to the darkness of sleep.

How does the Holy Spirit guarantee the blessings to come?

The essence of a tithe is to use a portion in order to secure greater blessings. To help us understand this we need to look at an aspect of the role played by the Holy Spirit in the history of salvation.

In Genesis 1 and 2 the Holy Spirit is mentioned twice:

'The earth was formless and void, with darkness over the abyss, and the Spirit of God hovered over the waters'

Gen. 1:2.

and,

'The Lord God formed man out of the clay of the ground and breathed into his nostrils the breath of life, so many became a living being'

Gen 2:7.

Gen 1:2 is a very mysterious verse, whereas Gen 2:7 is perhaps less so. The Spirit of God hovers over the waters that in verses six through to nine become God's focus of creation after he has first created light. In verse six he separates bodies of water and calls one of them 'sky' or, 'heaven'. Following this he gathers the waters under the sky together and forms the sea. As the Spirit of God hovers over the initial waters of chaos, eventually order and unity comes to these waters, God's creative Word is spoken and harmony is the fruit.

In Genesis 2:7 Adam is formed from the ground and is distinguished from all the wild animals by the breath, (Hebrew – *'neshamah'*) of life, (Hebrew – *'chayim',* pronounced with 'ch' as in 'chorus'). It is this breath of life – the Holy Spirit, which makes man a *'living being'.* He is the supreme creature that resembles the creator in whose image and likeness he is made. He is filled with God's Spirit to a point of overflowing, and is perfectly filled with grace in harmony with what God had in place for him.

The Spirit of God is the primary 'actor' on the stage of creation. God's Word appears less obvious because the narrative shows God *speaking* various elements into being without any clear declaration. The Father is not mentioned, nor is the Son, but the Spirit is explicit and it is he who brings life and makes man unique in the order of creation. When man sins, although he is immediately removed from Eden (Genesis 3:23), he does not lose the breath of life until we get to Genesis 6:3:

'My Spirit shall not remain in man forever since he is but flesh'

Man loses the breath of life – the Holy Spirit, as a result of his continuing in a state of sin, though it does take an apparently long time. God is patient with our sanctification, and patient with us when we fall into sin!

The Spirit of God is strongly connected with the waters of creation and with the creation and sanctification of the first man. Consequently, when man is 'recreated' as a result of Christ's death and resurrection, the same Spirit is central. When Mary conceives Jesus in the womb she visits her cousin Elizabeth. At the sound of her greeting Elizabeth, John the Baptist, the infant in Elizabeth's womb responds with a joyous movement; Elizabeth is filled with the Holy Spirit.

'When Elizabeth heard Mary's greeting, the infant leaped in her womb, and Elizabeth, filled with the Holy Spirit...'

Luke 1:41.

The standard Jewish greeting to this day is 'Shalom' which translates as 'peace'. So when Mary stands at the threshold to Elizabeth's house, which is the house of a descendant of Aaron, the great High Priest of Israel, she has the Word of God in her womb; she has God's Word in her heart (she is free from sin and thus God's Word consumes her heart); she touches the Word of God contained in the small box called a Mezuzah which is on the doorpost[#1] finally she proclaims God's Word, 'Shalom', at which point the Holy Spirit comes into Elizabeth and John the Baptist and fills them both.

In a way that reminds us of Genesis 2:7, the Lord on the day of resurrection appears to the disciples in the upper room and speaks the same word, 'Shalom' and the same thing happens:

'He breathed on them and said to them, "Receive the Holy Spirit'

John. 20:21.

Jesus first speaks the word of shalom, the peace that Adam would have known in the Garden of Eden because for a brief moment of time Adam and Eve lived in a beautiful shalom. When Jesus has destroyed the power of sin that is brought into the world through our first parents he restores shalom and brings to his disciples the same breath of life that he had breathed into the first man as he lay on the ground in the garden. On that first resurrection Sunday he has risen as a new Adam and gives to the disciples that which the first Adam should have passed to all generations (as opposed to original sin which is what he did pass). The disciples are filled with the breath of life and given the power to forgive sins. This is a reversal of the original sin that was discussed earlier in the chapter when Adam sinned. By disobeying God he committed the first sin and eventually lost the gift of the Holy Spirit. He died. Jesus changed all of this. He obeyed God, healed the wound of sin by suffering death for all, then gave the Holy Spirit with the power to forgive all sins. It is not *just* forgiveness of sins, but an outpouring of that same Spirit that hovered over the waters of creation.

When we have received the Holy Spirit, and daily open our lives to Him more and more, we access the promises of God and become richer for it.

'For in him every one of God's promises is a "Yes." For this reason it is through him that we say the "Amen," to the glory of God. But it is God who establishes us with you in Christ and has anointed us, by putting his seal on us and giving us his Spirit in our hearts as a first instalment'

2 Corinthians 1:20-22.

In Christ, every promise that God has made is a 'yes'. When we read the scriptures, whether it is the Old or the New Testament, whenever God makes a promise to an individual or a nation, that promise becomes a 'yes' for us in Christ. For example, many people are concerned for the lives of their children who have strayed from the faith and are living often very confused lives. Here is a promise from the Psalms which will be covered later in the book:

'Praise the LORD! Happy are those who fear the LORD, who greatly delight in his commandments. Their descendants will be mighty in the land; the generation of the upright will be blessed. Wealth and riches are in their houses, and their righteousness endures forever'

Psalm 112:1-3

The Psalm is stating that if a person fears the Lord their children will, become mighty, be blessed, and their righteousness will endure. All that is required is the fear of the Lord, a great grace that God is very willing to bestow. If a person prays for this grace (... and you can pray right now if you put the book down and spend a moment in silence before God), the blessings of this grace will overflow into your family and your children will have their lives changed – because of your relationship with God. Nonetheless, it is worth noting that sometimes this change may not happen in the lifetime of the parents. That is why faith is so important, we believe not because of what we see, but because of God's promises, even if those promises do not appear fulfilled in our lifetime on earth.

Saint Paul goes on to write that God has established us in relationship with him, anointed us with the Holy Spirit, sealed our soul (confirmation) so that we definitely belong to Christ, and he has given us the Spirit in our hearts as a first instalment. Once again, the language implies a deposit that guarantees blessing. Only when we grasp this principle will our hearts be free, enabling us to return to God a portion of that which he has given to us.

A personal witness

I never really gave a penny to the Church until I was filled with the Holy Spirit. My money was my hard-earned cash and as far as I was concerned the Church had plenty of cash and did not require my funds. In 1989 I started attending a charismatic prayer meeting in Acocks Green, Birmingham. The very first night I was so amazed with the freedom of the people as they worshipped God that I longed for what they had. God touched my heart and I began to experience freedom. I had a pound coin in my pocket and I generously gave it into a collection for tea/coffee! I felt free.

In February 1990 the same group prayed for me to be baptised in the Holy Spirit. I received the deposit that guarantees blessing (the Holy Spirit). Within a few weeks I cleared possessions out of my bedroom (I lived at home), including a record collection, video's, television, video recorder, books, and other bits. I gave them away to a jumble sale. I was in debt to the tune of £2,500 (I was earning about £6,000 per year so it was a large debt). I started tithing, which defied logic. Within a few months I had sold my car which was costing me a lot and received a company car. Within a year I got out of that £2,500 debt and had £2,000 in the bank. God had totally reversed my financial situation. It was the first time I had been out of debt since I got a credit card at the age of 19 and it was totally connected to my experience of being filled with the Holy Spirit. That is why this book is not just about cold, hard cash, but is a teaching on the Holy Spirit and Jesus.

It is no good me writing to you about tithing your money without getting to the source of why we do not tithe. We do not because we do not necessarily have an intimate relationship with Jesus Christ brought about through the power of the Holy Spirit. Before we have this relationship we will not be willing to contribute much to the Church. (There may be exceptions). Once we have experienced the power of the Holy Spirit we are set free from all sorts of things, and established in a more personal relationship with Christ. Consequently we are willing to put more into that relationship and this includes our cash. Some will give more than they had been, others will tithe, others will give more than a tithe (the sequence runs as tithe – gift – offering, or something like that). Either way, because we have had an intimate encounter with Christ we are liberated to live a more sacrificial life and are willing to invest more into the Body of Christ rather than into our own selfish indulgences.

In Acts 2:38, St Peter proclaims:

'Repent and be baptised, every one of you, in the name of Jesus Christ for the forgiveness of your sins; and you will receive the gift of the holy Spirit.'

In Acts 2:44, 45, those who had come into the community and were filled with the Holy Spirit had an extraordinary testimony made of their lives. They didn't just tithe!

'All who believed were together and had all things in common; they would sell their property and possessions and divide them among all according to each one's need.'

Such freedom and commitment to the Church is only possible through the power of the Holy Spirit. This is what we must pray for if we wish to be liberated from financial fears and experience the freedom of the children of God.

* * * * *

#1 Within the Mezuzah there is a small parchment containing the words of Dt. 6:4, *'Here O Israel, the Lord your God, the Lord is One. And you shall love the Lord your God with all of your heart, and all of your soul, and all of your strength'*

3. First Fruits

'But in fact Christ has been raised from the dead, the first fruits of those who have died.'

1 Corinthians 15:20.

In the New American Bible the footnote commenting on this verse reads, "The first fruits: the portion of the harvest offered in thanksgiving to God implies the consecration of the entire harvest to come. Christ's resurrection is not an end in itself; its finality lies in the whole harvest, ourselves." In other words, Saint Paul is using the analogy of the wheat harvest in reference to the resurrection. Not just the resurrection of Christ, but also ours at the end of time. Saint Paul is stating that the resurrection of Jesus is a guarantee that one day we will also be raised from the dead with an imperishable body. To show this he uses the phrase 'first fruits' which is the portion of the harvest that serves to consecrate the remainder that has not yet been harvested. Saint Paul also writes:

'We ourselves who have the first fruits of the Spirit...'

Romans 8:23.

Jesus is the first fruit of the resurrection. After his resurrection, which guarantees ours, he gives us the fruits of the Spirit. This guarantees our eternal inheritance. We need to spend a little time studying this, but first let us take a close look at the Hebrew word for 'first fruits'.

Reshith (beginnings/first fruit)

The Hebrew phrase for 'first fruits' is *reshith* and actually means 'beginnings' or 'first'. However, if we look at the root of the word there is a great deal of revelation to be had. The Bible in Hebrew begins with the word *bereshith,* which is generally translated as 'In the beginning.' In Revelation 21:6 and 22:13 Jesus declares:

'I am the Alpha and the Omega, the beginning and the end.'

If we apply this to Genesis 1:1, Jesus is the beginning in whom all things were created:

'In (Jesus) God (The Father) created the heavens and the earth.'

This is confirmed in Colossians 1:16, 17:

'For in him all things in heaven and on earth were created, things visible and invisible, whether thrones or dominions or rulers or powers—all things have been created through him and for him. He himself is before all things, and in him all things hold together.'

Thus, all things were created in Jesus, for Jesus, through Jesus, and are held together in Jesus. #2

Following this there is further revelation concerning the Trinity right at the beginning of God's Word:

'In the beginning when God created the heavens and the earth, the earth was a formless void and darkness covered the face of the deep, while a wind from God swept over the face of the waters.'

Genesis 1:2.

Unfortunately many Bible translations will render the Hebrew phrase *ruach elohim* as 'divine wind' or 'wind from God' as above in the New Revised Standard Version. However, the Douay Rheims translates the scripture as:

'The spirit of God moved over the waters.'

Thus, within the first two verses of the Bible there is a revelation of the Trinity that can be known only when we get to the last verses of the Bible, and we can read it as follows *(using the Douay Rheims version)*:

'In (Jesus – the logos) the beginning God (The Father) created heaven, and earth. And the earth was void and empty, and darkness was upon the face of the deep; and the Spirit of God (Holy Spirit) moved over the waters.'

Why is this important for our study of tithing?

As Jesus is the first fruits of the resurrection, and the Holy Spirit is the first fruits of our inheritance, in order to really get to grips with this we need to look in detail at the Jewish roots of our faith found in the Old Testament. The New Testament should not be understood without the Old Testament, nor should the Old Testament be understood until it is read in the light of the New Testament. So let us enjoy our study and plunge into the deep and vibrant waters of the living Word of God.

Beginnings

As stated earlier, the first word in the Bible is *bereshith* which can be used for Jesus as stated in Revelation 22. As an aside, the first word uttered in the scriptures is the only word uttered by the Father. According to the mystics the only word uttered by God the Father is 'Jesus' and everything he has to say is summed up in that Living Word.

If we take the word *bereshith* and take out *be* which gives us 'in the', we are left with 'beginnings', the word *reshith*. This is the Hebrew word for 'first fruits.' However, the Rabbis recommend going to the root of the word in order to glean a deeper meaning. Consequently, the root of *reshith* is *rosh* which has a multitude of meanings amongst which is *source, head, beginnings,* and *rivers.* The suggestion being 'the source of a river'. If we put this together the first word of the Bible, *bereshith* can be referring to the beginning or source of a river. Following this train of thought if we go to the last book of the Bible, and indeed, the final chapter, we find a river:

'Then the angel showed me the river of the water of life, bright as crystal, flowing from the throne of God and of the Lamb through the middle of the street of the city. On either side of the river is the tree of life with its twelve kinds of fruit, producing its fruit each month; and the leaves of the tree are for the healing of the nations.'

Revelation 22:1, 2.

There are a number of things in this paragraph to consider in the light of the book of Genesis. Obviously there is the 'river of the water of life'; this is the Holy Spirit which flows from the throne of God and of the Lamb. Thus the book of Revelation clearly shows us the source of the river which the book of Genesis gives us a suggestion of. In Genesis we find four rivers:

'A river flows out of Eden to water the garden, and from there it divides and becomes four branches.'

Genesis 2:10.

The Hebrew word for 'branches' in this translation is actually *rosh*, our root word from beginnings. So we have the river of life in the book of revelation, and we have the river watering the garden of Eden in Genesis. This latter river divides into four 'branches' or 'heads' which can once again be wonderfully viewed in the blazing light of the New Testament. The river flowing out of Eden is likened to the Holy Spirit which waters the garden of God. That river divides when it gets to the New Testament and brings us the four Gospels – the four branches of Good News which flow out into the world.

Going back to the book of Revelation, the river of life is sourced (*rosh*) in the throne of God and of the Lamb, thus the Holy Spirit is flowing from the throne of the Father and the Son. He brings life wherever he flows and we find on either side of the river the tree of life which brings healing. This is the same tree that God creates in the Garden of Eden:

'Out of the ground the LORD God made to grow every tree that is pleasant to the sight and good for food, the tree of life also in the midst of the garden.'

The book of proverbs, in describing *Wisdom,* tells us that:

'She is a tree of life to those who lay hold of her; those who hold her fast are called happy.'

Although it is referring to Wisdom in the feminine, Jesus is often referred to as wisdom personified, thus he is also, figuratively speaking, the Tree of life for us. Indeed, in the book of Revelation the tree of life brings healing, as does faith in Jesus.

Reshith *(First fruits)*

We got onto this exploration of Genesis because the Hebrew word for first fruits is *reshith* which is first found in Genesis 1:1. Now that we can appreciate that Jesus is the Beginning ... he is the *reshith*, we may be able to explore the nature of first fruits in the Old Testament. Remember that Jesus is present in the Old because this is a fundamental aspect of Old Testament study. We cannot divorce the second person of the Trinity from Old Testament revelation. In fact, the Father is not really found in the Old Testament except his creative touch in Genesis, he is transcendent and sends either the Son or the Spirit to perform various tasks. The Son is sent, (John 5:36) and the Spirit is sent, (John 14:26), but the Father is never sent and thus never directly intervenes in human affairs. The Fathers of the Church wrote on this topic. Those who wish to study it further can find it in St Justin Martyr, St Irenaeus, and St Clement.

Using what is known as 'typology' (finding a 'type' of Jesus in the Old Testament), we can study the following scriptures with new depth.

'The LORD spoke to Moses: Speak to the people of Israel and say to them: When you enter the land that I am giving you and you reap its harvest, you shall bring the sheaf of the first fruits of your harvest to the priest. He shall raise the sheaf before the LORD, that you may find acceptance; on the day after the sabbath the priest shall raise it.'

Leviticus 23:9-11.

This is the gift of the Passover that God gave the Israelites on Mount Sinai. The scripture speaks of Christ's resurrection and the harvest that comes from proclaiming Jesus crucified and risen (cf. 1 Corinthians 2:2). If we take Leviticus 23:9-11 and break it open line by line we read it like the following:

- Enter the Land – the Kingdom of God

- Reaping the harvest – the conversion of the nations

- Sheaf of first fruits – Jesus ('unless a grain of wheat', John 12:24).

- Raise the sheaf – Jesus resurrected.

- Finding acceptance – Now is the acceptable day (2 Corinthians 6:2).

- The day after the Sabbath – Sunday, the Lord's day, day of resurrection.

- The priest shall raise it – Christ, the Great High Priest, was given power to lay his life down, and power to take it up again (John 10:18).

Now I will paraphrase Leviticus 23:9-11 from the above:

When you *enter the Kingdom of God*, which I (God) am giving you as a gift, I want you to offer this to all the nations, make disciples of them also. The way to do this is to *raise up Jesus*, exalt him with your proclamation and your way of life. Consequently, you will be *acceptable to me through this act of obedience* and I will *grant your soul the rest it seeks.* Nonetheless all of this is the activity of Jesus in you and he is the one who *raises himself up* both in your heart and in the hearts of those whom you proclaim the Good News to. He is also the one who will give you rest.

There may be a touch of confusion because we are supposed to be discussing the feast of first fruits, yet here we have the 'sheaf of first fruits'. There is no contradiction. Immediately after the feast of Passover during the feast of Unleavened Bread, the Jewish farmer takes a sheaf of the first fruits, which is basically the first cutting, and presents it to the Lord in the temple. Note, this is the very first cutting of the harvest, it is also the best sheaf that can be found. In order for us to give effectively into God's Kingdom via the Church and various charities, we need to really grasp what is taking place at these various feasts. In reality the harvest has not actually begun. The fields are ripened by the time of Passover and are ready to be harvested. The farmer does not launch into the harvest, but takes a pilgrimage to Jerusalem and presents the best sheaf, the sheaf of first fruits. He presents in the temple as an offering to the Lord. One could call it the cream of the cream of the crop! It is not kept for sale in the market. It is not taken into the farmers house to be cooked when his best friends come for lunch. It is not offered to a local dignitary in order to curry favour. It is taken to the temple in Jerusalem in accordance with the Law that God gave, and offered to the Lord.

Why? This is a very pertinent question, but before we answer it here are a few more scriptures concerning this very important and very interesting happening.

'Go and proclaim in the hearing of Jerusalem, Thus says the LORD: I remember the devotion of your youth, your love as a bride, how you

followed me in the wilderness, in a land not sown. Israel was holy to the LORD, the first fruits of his harvest. All who ate of it were held guilty; disaster came upon them, says the LORD.'

Jeremiah 2:2, 3.

Jeremiah prophesies how God loved Israel's devotion as they wandered in the Sinai wilderness. In that time Israel was devoted to God and was called 'the first fruits' of his harvest. Israel was the first nation chosen by God to serve him. The rest of the nations were invited to participate in this sovereign choice after the resurrection when Jesus sends out his disciples. However, before that happened, all who attacked Israel, who were seen to 'eat of the first fruits' had disaster come upon them. The first fruits belonged to God and if anybody tried to take them they suffered as a result.

'He commanded the people who lived in Jerusalem to give the portion due to the priests and the Levites, so that they might devote themselves to the law of the LORD. As soon as the word spread, the people of Israel gave in abundance the first fruits of grain, wine, oil, honey, and of all the produce of the field; and they brought in abundantly the tithe of everything.'

2 Chronicles 31:4, 5.

This scripture refers to the time of King Hezekiah who brings about something of a revival in Israel. Other kings had given the land over to worship of idols, but Hezekiah reverses this trend. Among other things he wants to restore the temple worship, and in order to achieve this he wants the priests to devote themselves to the law (Hebr. *Torah*) of the LORD. When the word spread the people brought in the first fruits and the tithe of everything. This enabled the priests and Levites to function accordingly.

'We obligate ourselves to bring the first fruits of our soil and the first fruits of all fruit of every tree, year by year, to the house of the LORD.'

Nehemiah 10:35

In this case the Israelites have been exiled to Babylon for seventy years. Nehemiah was with the returning exiles who came across the books of the Law and read them to the people. They were in the process of applying various Laws and this was one of the obligations they took upon themselves. By obeying the ordinance of the first fruits they hope to bring God's blessing down upon themselves. Indeed, this is exactly what would happen. Obedience brings blessing.

It is an interesting scenario that the Jews enjoyed a pre-exile revival which enabled them to enjoy harvest and bring in first fruits to the temple. During the exile there was no temple worship, thus they could not bring in the first fruits, then this is restored when they return from exile and read from the Torah.

It could be argued that England is in a similar situation today. Before the reformation it was a legal requirement to bring in a tithe, and we still have tithe barns around the country standing as a testimony to this. This all changed at the reformation from 1538 when Henry VIII had himself made head of the Church of England. For nearly 500 years this has been the case. In the 19th century the Catholic hierarchy was re-established in England and is ready to bear fruit. St Edward the Confessor, formerly patron Saint of England, had a vision on his deathbed of the reformation. He concluded that the Church would again be joined to Rome and bear much fruit.

So, why? What is the point of the Jewish farmer bringing in the first fruits of his harvest to the temple and offering them to God for consumption by the Priests and Levites? Obviously, there was a reason for God asking this of the Jewish farmer. However, a further answer lies in the New Testament.

Saint Paul writes concerning the first fruits:

'For as all die in Adam, so all will be made alive in Christ. But each in his own order: Christ the first fruits, then at his coming those who belong to Christ.'

1 Corinthians 15:22, 23.

Once again, Paul identifies Christ as the first fruits. The first fruits are no longer seen as a sheaf, or sheafs, of wheat, but now they are a person. Referring to his death and resurrection Christ said:

'Unless a grain of wheat falls into the ground and dies, it remains but a single grain. But if it dies it yields much fruit.'

John 12:24.

Now we can begin to see how Jesus fulfils the Law.

Saint Paul takes us back to the first man with another reference to the first fruits:

'If the part of the dough offered as first fruits is holy, then the whole batch is holy; and if the root is holy, then the branches also are holy.'

Romans 11:16

The first man was Adam. He sinned and consequently humanity inherited that original sin and all men fell from grace into bondage. Thus the 'first fruits' of humanity was corrupted, and so all of humanity was corrupted. We needed a new 'first fruits'. Israel fulfils that, prophetically being called God's first fruits.

From Israel would come the Messiah, Jesus the Son of God. He is the 'sheaf of first fruits', the first fruits of the resurrection. He is the first sheaf plucked from the harvest of humanity, pure and holy, completely without sin, having carried away the sin of the world, and he is offered to the Father as an unblemished sacrifice. He renews the whole of humanity and gives us a new foundation, new roots. Indeed, Saint Paul writes:

'That you, rooted and grounded in love ...'

Ephesians 3:17

Before Christ all peoples were rooted and grounded in sin. Once Christ redeems us and we are baptised, then we are 'rooted and grounded in love'. The roots are now holy and so the branches (us) are found to be holy.

However, Paul does not just call Christ the first fruits. We share in his inheritance.

'But we must always give thanks to God for you, brothers and sisters beloved by the Lord, because God chose you as the first fruits for salvation through sanctification by the Spirit and through belief in the truth.'

2 Thessalonians 2:13

This can also be translated as, 'God chose you from the beginning' which echoes the earlier study of this word which translates as, 'beginnings'. Our salvation was arranged from the beginning, as a first fruit if you like.

'In fulfilment of his own purpose he gave us birth by the word of truth, so that we would become a kind of first fruits of his creatures.'

James 1:18

The New American Bible footnotes have the following comment on this scripture:

'Acceptance of the Gospel message, the word of truth, constitutes new birth and makes the recipient the firstfruits (i.e. the cultic offering of the earliest

grains, symbolizing the beginning of an abundant harvest) of a new creation.'

Note that it says 'first fruits of his creatures'. This suggests that we are the first to be redeemed. Isaiah implies that the rest of creation will also be redeemed in some fashion:

'Then the wolf shall be a guest of the lamb, and the leopard shall lie down with the kid; The calf and the young lion shall browse together, with a little child to guide them.'

Isaiah 11:6

And Saint Paul:

'Creation itself would be set free from slavery to corruption and share in the glorious freedom of the children of God.'

Romans 8:21

When the first man, Adam, sinned, the entire creation fell into decay. Humanity first, then animals and the rest of creation. Christ came as the second Adam to redeem humanity because we are the peak of visible creation (fallen angels cannot be redeemed, their choice is fixed for ever) And then, through us as the first fruits of the redemption, the rest of creation is consecrated and ready to be redeemed at the appropriate time. This is why first fruits are so important. They consecrate the remainder of the batch.

Finally, in the book of Revelation it is stated explicitly who the first fruits belong to:

'They have been redeemed from humankind as first fruits for God and the Lamb.'

Revelation 14:4

And the last word in this chapter goes to the wisdom of Sirach:

'Fear the Lord and honour the priest, and give him his portion, as you have been commanded: the first fruits, the guilt offering, the gift of the shoulders, the sacrifice of sanctification, and the first fruits of the holy things. Stretch out your hand to the poor, so that your blessing may be complete. Give graciously to all the living; do not withhold kindness even from the dead.'

Sirach 7:31-33

* * * * *

#2 Jesus is present at creation as the Eternal Word and Second Person of the Blessed Trinity. The Church Fathers would often refer to the pre-incarnate Christ as the 'Logos': (John 1:1), 'In the beginning was the Word (Gk, *logos*) and the Word (*logos*) was with God, and the Word (*logos*) was God.'

4: Pentecost

(Feast of weeks, feast of first fruits)

This is one of the few feasts that is observed by Jews and 'Gentiles' (Christians specifically) alike. It is also the feast when we bring in the 'tithe'. Thus, it gets its own chapter.

• The feast of Pentecost was a Jewish festival for over 1000 years before Christianity was born.

• Pentecost is not a separate feast to Easter. It concludes the Easter celebration. We could say that Pentecost is to Easter what the feast of the Epiphany is to Christmas.

Just as the Epiphany can be lost in the materialistic 'razzmatazz' that surrounds Christmas, so can Pentecost be lost in the aftermath of Easter. The feast of Pentecost is called *'Shavuot'* by Jews. Shavuot is a Hebrew word meaning 'weeks' because there are seven weeks from the Passover to Pentecost. The Rabbis tells us that Shavuot is the concluding feast to Passover. There is then an intrinsic link between these two festivals.

This is not just Hebrew thinking. The Catholic Catechism states:

'On the day of Pentecost when the seven weeks of Easter had come to an end,

Christ's Passover is fulfilled in the outpouring of the Holy Spirit.[#3]

The fulfilment of the death and resurrection of Christ is found in the feast of Pentecost when Jesus sends the Spirit.

There is a reason the two feasts are linked so closely:

'I will be with you; and this shall be your proof that it is I who have sent you: when you bring my people out of Egypt, you will worship God on this very mountain.'

Exodus 3:12.

In this passage of scripture God's first comment is echoed in Matthew 28:20 when he tells his disciples he will be with them always. God then goes on to give Israel a 'sign' or 'proof' of his presence with them. The 'sign' of God's presence is 'you will worship God on this very mountain.' Jewish thought indicates that the Jews are not being liberated from Egypt to do whatever they want; they are being liberated to worship and serve God. True freedom is not being able to do what we want, it is being free to say 'yes' to God. Sin is doing whatever we want to do. It is what we would call selfishness. Left to our own devices we will fall rapidly into sin as demonstrated by our first parents. The sign that God is with Israel at the Exodus is they will be led from slavery in Egypt to freedom at Sinai.

The feast of Pentecost is about a manifestation or an experience of true freedom. Exodus 3:12 connects Passover with Pentecost. It points towards the slavery of the Jews in Egypt which ends with Passover (when you bring my people out of Egypt) and it concludes with Israel gathering around Mount Sinai at Pentecost, *'you will worship God on this very mountain'*.

Physically, the Israelites journeyed from Egypt to Sinai, whilst spiritually they are journeying from slavery to freedom. This is also symbolised by the two feasts. Passover is celebrated whilst they are in slavery but it sets them free; Pentecost is first celebrated at Mount Sinai when they receive the commandments which give them their pathway not just to freedom, but to remaining free. Egypt symbolises a slavery to sin, whereas the desert journey symbolises their pathway to growing in holiness.

The first Pentecost

'Moses then turned and came down the mountain with the two tablets of the commandments in his hands, tablets that were written on both sides, front and back; tablets that were made by God, having inscriptions on them that were engraved by God himself.'

Exodus 32:15, 16

Pentecost was a feast on which the Jews celebrated the giving of the Law to Moses on Sinai. Consequently it is considered to be the birthday of Judaism. The above scripture tells us that Moses brought the Law, or Torah, down from Mount Sinai and this was traditionally said to be the first Pentecost. As previously stated, but in order to get greater emphasis:

At Passover the Jews gain their freedom from slavery.

At Pentecost they receive the Law which enables them to remain free.

This statement regarding the Law setting them free is not entirely true. The Catholic Catechism states:

'God gave the Law as a 'pedagogue' to lead his people toward Christ. But the Law's

powerlessness to save man deprived of the divine 'likeness'... enkindles a desire for the

Holy Spirit.'

The purpose of the Law was to manifest the power of sin (cf. Rom. 3:20). It showed that man was held captive by sin. As man realises this he begins to desire freedom, which comes when the Spirit is sent.

At 'Passover' (Easter) Christians are set free from sin by the saving death and resurrection of Jesus Christ. At Pentecost Christians receive power from on high which enables us to stay free from the power of sin and grow in holiness.

'These words, and nothing more, the LORD spoke with a loud voice to your entire assembly on the mountain from the midst of the fire and the dense cloud. He wrote them upon two tablets of stone and gave them to me.'

Deuteronomy 5:22.

When God gave Moses the Torah it was on Mount Sinai, from the midst of the fire, written by God's finger on both sides of two tablets of stone. It was written in Hebrew.

The Catholic Catechism says this regarding fire:

'Fire symbolizes the transforming energy of the Holy Spirit's actions. The prayer of the Prophet Elijah, who 'arose like fire' and whose 'word burned like a torch,' brought down fire from heaven on the sacrifice on Mount Carmel. This event was a 'figure' of the fire of the Holy Spirit, who transforms what he touches. Jesus will say of the Spirit: 'I came to cast fire upon the earth; and would that it were already kindled!'

The spiritual tradition has retained this symbolism of fire as one of the most expressive images of the Holy Spirit's actions.[#4]

The Catechism also refers to God's writing of the Law:

'If God's law was written on tablets of stone 'by the finger of God', then the 'letter from

Christ' entrusted to the care of the apostles is written 'with the Spirit of the living God, not on tablets of stone, but on tablets of human hearts'. The hymn Venn Creator

Spiritus invokes the Holy Spirit as the 'finger of the Father's right hand".

Consequently in Deuteronomy 5 we can see that God's fire is a manifestation of the Holy Spirit, and the 'finger' that God used to write the law is the Holy Spirit. God's Word is being written by the power of God's Spirit.

The feast of Pentecost

Three names are given in the scriptures for the feast of Pentecost:-

• 'The Feast of (Seven) Weeks' because it is seven 'weeks' after Passover (Exodus 34:22).

• 'Pentecost' (Greek for 'The Fiftieth'), because it is on the fiftieth day after Passover (Leviticus 23:16).

• 'The Feast of First fruits' as it is the day on which the Jews bring into the temple the 'first fruits' of the harvest (Numbers 28:26)

The feast of Pentecost was a thanksgiving feast at the end of the grain harvest which began at Passover. Later tradition made it a commemoration of the giving of the law at Sinai. As previously stated, the first Pentecost is traditionally the day on which Moses descends from Mount Sinai with the Word of God. Pentecost is fulfilled on the day when the Holy Spirit descended from God's holy mountain to write the Word of God on our hearts. However, these are the word that God gives to Moses regarding the offering to be given on the first Pentecost:

'For the wave offering of your first fruits to the LORD, you shall bring with you from wherever you live two loaves of bread made of two tenths of an Stephan of fine flour and baked with leaven.'

Leviticus 23:17.

The loaves are baked with leaven which symbolizes sin. This is because leaven was used to puff up the bread in a similar way to how pride puffs up the person. For the Passover feast unleavened bread was used pointing to Christ who is without sin, and the victory of the cross when the power of sin is defeated. At Pentecost the outpouring of the Holy Spirit is over the church ... onto a group of people who still have sin in them (like leaven in bread), but the sin no longer has power over them. We are those people. Although we still 'fall' into sin, it does not have the hold over our lives that we may think it does. When Catholics 'fall' into sin we confess our sins to a priest who can absolve us from it. Sin has no power over us.

The fine flour that is used to bake the bread is like the dust from which we were made:

'from dust you came and to dust you shall return'

(Genesis 3:19)

This is our flesh, our bodies, which become temples of the Holy Spirit.

(cf. 1 Cor. 6:19)

The two loaves of bread offered to God foreshadow the Jews and Gentiles who can both come into the presence of God as from the day of Pentecost. Until that time only one person a year could enter into the presence of God, the High Priest on the Feast of the Atonement *(see the chapter on Tabernacles).* Jesus has defeated the power of sin and poured out his Spirit, so that all people can approach God. That is why the veil of the temple was torn in two when Jesus died. The way is now open.

'Besides the bread, you shall offer to the LORD a holocaust of seven unblemished yearling lambs, one young bull, and two rams, along with their cereal offering and libations, as a sweet-smelling oblation to the LORD.'

Leviticus 23:18.

All of this is meaningful and points towards Jesus as the Lamb of God and the ram who is slain. The seven unblemished, yearling lambs also foreshadow Jesus. The lambs are unblemished meaning they are perfect, which is like Jesus who is without sin and thus morally perfect. The word 'yearling' can also be translated as 'one year old'. A literal rendering of yearling is:

'Hannah'

To change, disguise

This alludes to Jesus who disguised his glory and walked among us as one of us. The young bull foreshadows Jesus who is the servant king. The two rams point towards the two natures Jesus held, the human and the divine. He was fully human and fully divine.

The priest takes our offering and brings it before the LORD.

'These shall be sacred to the LORD and belong to the priest.'

Leviticus 23:20

This ultimately speaks of a person who has been baptised in the Holy Spirit and is a member of the Body of Christ. They are sacred and belong to Christ (the priest).

'Now those who belong to Christ (Jesus) have crucified their flesh with its passions and desires.'

Galatians 5:24.

To summarise Leviticus 23:15-22, the central elements of Pentecost include:

• A day of rest.

• Two loaves of bread are offered which are made with fine flour and baked with leaven. The two loaves can represent the Jews and Gentiles. The bread symbolises our flesh. The leaven symbolizes the sinful nature. The fine flour symbolizes dust, (cf. Genesis 3:19)

• Pentecost is the birthday of Judaism and the Church.

• This is also called the Feast of First Fruits. It is the day on which the Hebrew Farmer brings into the temple the choicest First Fruit of his harvest. This action consecrates the remaining harvest to God and is symptomatic of our covenant relationship with God which calls us to bring the best that we have before God as a freewill gift.

The instructions for Pentecost are repeated in Numbers 28:26-31 where the people are told:

'You shall hold a sacred assembly, and do no sort of work.'

This is a foreshadowing of the Pentecost of Acts 2. The New Jerusalem Bible refers to 'an offering of new fruits' which is directing us to the Apostles gathered in the upper room. This gathering is a 'sacred assembly,' or as some translations would call it, 'a holy convocation'.

Deuteronomy 16:10 gives us the last reading of Pentecost from the Torah. It specifically connects the measure of our offering with the proportion of the blessing that God will give:

'You shall then keep the feast of Weeks in honour of the LORD, your God, and the measure of your own freewill offering shall be in proportion to the blessing the LORD, your God, has bestowed on you.'

In Acts 2:38 we are invited to 'repent' and 'receive the Holy Spirit'. Our relationship with God is a two-way process. God will pour out blessing into our lives, but his blessing demands a response from us. As we bring our offering into the presence of God, he will bless us. Our offering is ourselves. We bring our lives to God which is our act of repentance. The Greek word for repent is *'metanoia'* which means to change one's mind, to change the direction that one's life is going in.

To change one's mind about something means a change of heart. For example, if my mind is set on walking down a mountain, then I have a change of mind, turn around and start walking up that same mountain: the change of mind has caused a change of direction in my behaviour. This is what it means to repent; if a person is walking away from God as a result of their life choices, they repent by changing their life choices and turn back to God. If people are walking away from God they cannot receive the blessings God wants to pour into their heart. Once they turn back to God they can become recipients of His blessings.

God wills to pour into our hearts a blessing and invites us to give to him in proportion to what he has given us. As God has given us his only begotten Son, we should offer ourselves fully to Him:

'The measure of your own freewill offering shall be in proportion to the blessing the LORD, your God, has bestowed on you.'

Deuteronomy 16:10

Deuteronomy 16:11 tells us what to do in God's presence on this special occasion:

'In the place which the LORD, your God, chooses as the dwelling place of his name, you shall make merry in his presence'

In Acts 2:13 the Apostles behaviour causes onlookers to accuse them:

'But others said, scoffing, 'They have had too much new wine.'

The Apostles were 'making merry' or 'rejoicing' in the Lord's presence after they had received the Holy Spirit which caused them to behave as if they had drunk too much new wine. It is this outpouring of the Holy Spirit which dramatically changes the Apostles and this is something we need to seriously consider for our own lives. Firstly, prior to this event they locked themselves in the upper room for 'fear of the Jews'. Secondly, they were divided amongst themselves following the crucifixion, and Thomas refused to believe in the unanimous testimony of the Apostles. In other words, they were not free. Remember, the original purpose for Pentecost according to the book of Exodus was for us to be set free. That freedom enables us to give of ourselves into God's Kingdom. If we do not have that freedom, a gift granted by God, we cannot, or will not, give into His Kingdom.

When the Spirit came upon the Apostles the change could not be more dramatic. Not only are they released from their fears, but they appear on the streets with such abandon to the power of God's Spirit that the onlookers (who were there to bring in their first fruit offering – their tithe), were astounded and started mocking these men (and probably a few women).

We must remember when reading this narrative that Jews and Gentile converts have gathered for Pentecost from all over the known world. Jerusalem would be heaving with people who would most likely be very similar to the same crowds that had gathered for the Passover and seen the crucifixion.

So, not only are the Apostles completely abandoned to the power of the Spirit and thus have forgotten their fears, but they are also unashamed to publicly proclaim the Gospel that previously they had a very poor idea of. (Peter even said to Jesus, 'are you going to restore the Kingdom to Israel?'). This outpouring of the Spirit had turned their hearts around completely, and the Holy Spirit has been doing that same work for nearly two thousand years in the life of the Church, and He is going to be doing it even more in the coming years for this time of evangelization.

Once Peter has proclaimed the Gospel and 3000 men are added to their number something powerful happens:

'All who believed were together and had all things in common; they would sell their property and possessions and divide them among all according to each one's need.'

Acts 2: 44, 45.

One could almost say that rather than bringing in a tithe of their goods, the earliest Christianity community experiences a total commitment whereby those who have possessions give them all over for the Gospel … one hundred percent.

This is the action of the holy spirit

I have to write that in bold letters, because when we see that each week so many Catholics and Christians of various denominations are giving precious little to the Body of Christ, such that we cannot fulfil the evangelization mission of the Church. Yet, when the Spirit comes people want to give in to this work, as is testified at many Churches where they have a certain focus on the power of the Holy Spirit (see examples of tithing in the introduction). When a person has had an experience of the Holy Spirit it is so liberating that they have their eyes opened and one of the fruits is to 'give' into the missionary life of the Church. Specifically, that of evangelization, – the reason why the church exists.

'It is not right for us to neglect the word of God to serve at table'

Acts 6:2.

Indeed, Pope Paul VI wrote that the Church has had the single aim of fulfilling her duty of

being the messenger of the Good News of Jesus Christ. He went to further explain that 'the presentation of the Gospel message is not an optional contribution for the Church. It is the duty incumbent on her by the command of the Lord Jesus, so that people can believe and be saved. This message is indeed necessary. It is unique. It cannot be replaced. It does not permit either indifference, syncretism or accommodation. It is a question of people's salvation.' These are very strong words and they should motivate us to present our tithe to the Church so that souls can be saved. One could say, money can be given in order that souls can be saved. Who would have thought that?

In conclusion, it is most extraordinary that the feast God chooses as the one when we give of our produce into the Kingdom, is the very same feast that God chooses to send us the Spirit enabling us to be free enough to give even more – and freely.

* * * * *

#3 Catechism of the Catholic Church Article 731

#4 Catechism of the Catholic Church Article 696

5. Judaism and Tithing

'You shall eat in the presence of the LORD your God, at the place where He chooses to establish His name, he tithe of your grain, your new wine, your oil, and the firstborn of your herd and your flock, so that you may learn to fear the LORD your God always.'

Deuteronomy 14:23

When it comes to tithing, we can learn a lot from Judaism, which understands that the bringing in of the tithe is a direct request from God Himself. Furthermore, the Catholic Church teaches that the Word of God is inspired, it is 'God-breathed' to quote Saint Paul in his letter to Timothy. This includes the whole canon of scripture, including texts that invite the Jewish people to tithe. What is more, it belongs to that portion of the scriptures known as the Torah which has a special significance. Indeed, at the time of Jesus some Jewish leaders believed that only the Torah was inspired by God.

Tithing in the Torah

We have done a study of Abraham and Jacob elsewhere, so here I am going to focus on the Law that God gave to Moses in the wilderness, specifically the book of Leviticus where God tells Moses:

'Thus, all the tithe of the land, of the seed of the land or of the fruit of the tree, is the Lord's;

it is holy to the Lord.'

Leviticus 27:30

I point out that the book of Leviticus is very important. It is the third book of the Bible and thus the heart of the Torah. It is considered the heart of the Torah partly because every chapter, and sometimes within the chapters, it begins:

'The Lord said to Moses...'

The entire book is virtually a dictation from the Lord to Moses. It is also the book of holiness because frequently God tells Moses *'it is holy to the Lord'* in respect of the various groupings that are used. For example, in the above scripture regarding tithing God makes it clear that the tithe is holy to the Lord! What does this mean?

The Hebrew word for holy is *qadosh*. It means to be set apart for a purpose. Conversely the Hebrew word for profane is *choi*. That word means 'ordinary'. The distinction is that what is holy cannot be used for something ordinary. If something is *qadosh*, it cannot be used as *choi*. This is what happened in Leviticus 8. Previously, Aaron and Moses had offered a sacred sacrifice to God and fire came down and consumed the sacrifice. Then along come two of Aaron's sons and they offer their own sacrifice, without reference to God or the Law. The fruit of this is the fire once more came from God's presence, but this time the sons were consumed because they offered a profane sacrifice.

For Catholics the chalice used for the wine which is transformed into the precious blood of Jesus is also sacred. It would not be used for beer because it would be sacrilegious, to take that which is sacred and use it for something ordinary. One other aspect of this matter is the human body. For Christians our bodies are sacred and set aside for Christ:

'Do you not know that your body is a temple of the Holy Spirit who is in you, whom you have from

God, and that you are not your own.'

1 Corinthians 6:19

Therefore, we cannot use our bodies for sinful purposes, but if we profess the Christian faith, we must use our body for the glory of God. We are *qadosh*, set aside for the purpose and glory of God. To be frank, anything else would be destructive and lead to death anyway!

Tithing is a sacrifice, it is part of the Jewish sacrifice system. There is a communal purpose to the act of tithing in that it went to the Levites who served the Lord in the temple as a full-time occupation, so it supplied their needs. However, this is because of God's commandment regarding the tithe. The tithe is holy to the Lord, so if an individual takes that which belongs to God and uses it for their own benefit, that is called profane and it leads to death. On the other hand, if somebody gives the tithe into the 'storehouse', it can go to the minister of God and is a sacred offering.

When I was in full-time ministry as an Evangelist I had a number of people give me tithes, sometimes on a regular basis, sometimes they would give me a tithe of a bonus or an inheritance. These were incredibly faith-filled people who wanted to see the Church fulfil its mission of evangelisation and therefore they gave to somebody who was fully involved in that ministry. At that time it was me. Those tithes, together with the many offerings that I received from others, kept me going and enabled the Gospel to be preached in what I hoped was a powerful and effective manner to many souls.

Due to the sacred nature of the donations I was given I would always pray over the offerings people gave to me. Once when I was doing this, (actually, a number of times whilst I prayed over the money that had been given), people would run to the front and give more because I was praying a blessing over all of their finances. This is hugely important. If we give to God the sacred portion which is his due, then the remaining funds are also blessed. If we withhold that which belongs to God, then the rest is also profane!

The prayer I made over the offering would go along these lines. I would hold the offering in one hand, and place the other hand over the offering, then I would pray: 'Lord, please bless this offering. In the name of your Son, Jesus, I break all financial curses over our lives, I pray a blessing on all of our finances, our houses, our families, our harvests. I pray you pour out your Spirit on our families and all of our works, because we bring in to you the sacred portion – that which belongs to you, and you promise to open the floodgates of blessing upon our lives.'

I once spoke at a conference in Perth, Australia, and when the offering was brought to me I started praying and the music ministry started worshipping, so my prayer went on for some time – about 5 minutes or more. When they had counted the offering there was more in that one that in any of the others – quite probably more than the others combined! They also sold far more CD's that weekend than they would normally do. And one of those teachings touched quite heavily on tithing.

Even the tithe has to be tithed, so my wife and I would always tithe the offerings we received. When I was in Portugal leading a healing retreat some years ago, at the end of the retreat they gave me the offering, and I decided to tithe it back to them. It was a funny situation. As soon as they gave me the donation for the weekend, because it was cash I was able to feed 10% straight back into their ministry. The reaction was funny because they didn't quite know how to respond! No response is necessary, it is a tithe, a gift from God – the sacred portion.

The Levites were commanded to do the same:

'You shall speak to the Levites and say to them, 'When you take from the sons of Israel the tithe which I have given you form them for your inheritance, then you shall present an offering from it to the LORD, a tithe of the tithe.'

Numbers 18:26

How many of us have been given a specific personal command from God to tithe? Quite often we are told that tithing is unnecessary and not a healthy practice. Many may say to give 10% of our income to evangelisation is not a wise move. To a certain extent I can understand the argument. If we were tithing into evangelisation we may not see much of a return on our gift. It is not like going on a shopping trip whereby we exchange money for goods and we see the immediate return on our investment via goods, food, clothing, etc. The counter argument may be that we spend so much of our income on our own self-indulgence that our financial stewardship may not be considered wise, given that wisdom is a fruit of the Holy Spirit. Indeed, the wisdom of God is considered foolishness in this world (cf. 1 Corinthians 1:25), and the wise man of God is the one who would give his fullness to God in every respect.

If God issues a commandment that the tithe is sacred, it belongs to him, it is holy to Him, and that if we don't bring in the full tithe we come under a curse, then I would suggest that a more prayerful discernment of this method of financial giving is necessary. I wouldn't worry too much about foolish spending, we in the western world are expert at that already. What we need is more Godly wisdom.

Offerings

In the Torah, particularly the book of Leviticus, the Jews are given a number of offerings for a variety of circumstances. These are varied and consist of peace, thank (eucharistic), sin, and burnt offerings (Hebr. *olah*). The latter is my favourite because the rest tend to be given for a specified purpose to do with the offerer. For example, the sin offering is made because the person making the offering has sinned. However, the burnt offering is given for one specific reason, to give glory and praise to God. Also, nothing remains of the offering, it is burned up, or consumed entirely by fire. It is called the 'burnt offering' and the full description for it can be found in Leviticus 1. It is perhaps the most frequent offering in the Old Testament, but whenever you read about the 'burnt offering' remember it is being made for one purpose alone – to render glory and praise to God. One could say it is fulfilled in Acts 2 when the fire of God is poured out on the Apostles and they become a burnt offering. It is also fulfilled whenever the people of God burn with the fire of God's love and give their lives for his praise and glory.

The tithe is not one of these offerings, but it is an offering of the produce of the land or the livestock. On the other hand most of the other offerings tend to be from the livestock. The tithe is also there to benefit the Priests who minister in the temple in Jerusalem.

I don't want to go into the other offerings in depth in this chapter, if anything the purpose was to put tithing in a context of a broader system of sacrifices that were somewhat obligatory for the Jews from the time of Moses onwards. As Catholics we have a bit of a poor concept of sacrificial giving and our Church suffers for it. Many Catholics do give to the Body of Christ very generously, but they are certainly in the minority when one looks at the accounts of a parish or diocese. On the other hand, if Catholics could gain an understanding of sacrificial giving, and therefore tithing was just a part of that gift, our Church's finances could be transformed.

Do not be misled or deceived into thinking the Catholic Church is wealthy. It does a huge amount of good with preciously little resources and depends greatly on an army of voluntary workers, low paid staff, stipendiary-based religious and clergy, and very poor religious orders.

When the Church proclaims evangelical poverty it does so from its own experience and expertise.

* * * * *

6. Floodgates in Heaven

"Return to Me, and I will return to you,'says the LORD of hosts.

'But you say, 'How shall we return?"

Malachi 3:7

In the above scripture, God is calling the people of Israel to return to his presence after they have repeatedly turned aside from his teachings, what the Jews call the Torah. The agreement that God wants with his people is 'if you return to me I will return to you'. However, the people of God do not understand how they can return to Him so he has to give them something concrete that they can do in order to enjoy a spiritual revival. In answer to 'how shall we return' God responds:

'Will anyone rob God? Yet you are robbing me!'

Malachi, 3:8

God first lays down what he wants to do with his people *('return ... I will return')* and they respond by asking 'how?' Then he points out that they are 'robbing him'. Now there is an issue. How can we rob God? Perhaps we think that robbing God means invading his kingdom and taking his household treasures, as would be so in a normal robbery. In one sense this is true, however, in this scenario God wants to show us something else – keeping that which does not belong to us! In a sense this is tantamount to fiddling one's taxes, where one keeps that which belongs to HMRC. Thus, the people of God respond sensibly:

'But you say, 'How are we robbing you?"

Indeed, how are we robbing God? We obviously cannot take something off him, but we can withhold something from him!

'In your tithes and offerings! You are cursed with a curse, for you are robbing me – the whole nation of you!'

Malachi 3:9

By not bringing in tithes and offerings to God the nation has brought a curse down upon itself – 'cursed with a curse'. Now remember, this is part of the process that God will use in order to restore Israel as his people, *('return to me')*, so that God can be Israel's God *('I will return to you')*. In a sense, God is returning to Israel by raising up the prophet so that he can call Israel back. It is extraordinary that in order to re-establish the relationship with his people God would ask for the tithes and offerings to be restored. However, this is not just about bringing in the 10%, but also the condition of heart. The heart has to return to God but cannot do so if it is focussed on 'money' so to speak. Thus, the prophet Malachi proclaims the Word of God:

'Bring the full tithe into the storehouse, so that there may be food in my house, and thus put me to the test, says the LORD of hosts; '

Malachi 3:9

The physical storehouse is the temple of God in Jerusalem where God wants the Israelites to bring in their tithe of grain, etc, in order that there will be sufficient food to feed the hungry. When the people of God bring in the tithe there will be food in the house of God. There would be nothing worse than no food in God's house. Imagine, when we buy food from the local supermarket all is good, but when there is a problem people turn to the Church. In recent times many Churches have had food banks which have been overwhelmed. The worst-case scenario is not just the shops running out of food, but also the Church! Ironically a similar thing happened at the time of the English reformation when King Henry VIII destroyed the monasteries and convents. Monastic lands were seized by the state which then gave the crown a gross income of £300,000 per year (at the monetary rate in 1538). Some 318 small religious houses were closed by Oliver Cromwell, soon followed by major monasteries. Lead was stripped from the roofs of the monasteries and melted down. Jewels and plates were confiscated and sent to Henry's treasury. The land was redistributed to enrich the nobility that were loyal to Henry VIII.[5] The people who suffered as a result of the English reformation were the peasants who greatly depended on the land, and the food distribution from the religious houses.

Taking this a step further, the narrative proclaims, 'you are under a curse!' The curse is probably that there is no food in the house of God and that curse overflows into the nation where there are barren fields and no fruit on the vine; the locust devours the crop. This is clearly seen in the quote regarding the English reformation above. It can be seen that the nation came under a curse. Perhaps, in order to cure the problem all that the people have to do is bring in the tithe of whatever harvest they manage to get, then this happens:[6]

"See if I will not open the windows of heaven for you and pour down for you an overflowing blessing. I will rebuke the locust for you, so that it will not destroy the produce of your soil; and your vine in the field shall not be barren,' says the LORD of hosts. 'Then all nations will count you happy, for you will be a land of delight,' says the LORD of hosts"

Ml 3:11, 12.

The windows of heaven at the time of the flood were sufficient to flood the world. Indeed, the hebrew word for 'windows' is that used at the time of the flood when the 'floodgates' of the sky were opened to such a degree that the whole earth was flooded. However, in Malachi the word is being used in the context of blessing. In other words, God wants to completely flood our lives. By bringing in the whole tithe,

God promises that the 'floodgates' will be opened once again, flooding our lives in blessing with such an extravagant blessing that we will 'overflow'. The Hebrew rendering is that there will not be 'room enough' for all the blessings. Contrast that with the previous scripture where the nation is under a curse, to having so much blessing they do not have sufficient space available for storing the blessings, be they material or spiritual. The fulcrum on which this balances is the bringing in of a tithe.

Why is the tithe so important? It is obviously not important to God in respect of having an impact on him, because God is unchanging. Anything that we 'give' to him does not change him. It is well known that anything we supposedly do for God really changes us and those around us, not Him. The bringing in of the tithe is for our benefit, not God's! e wants to give us blessing, but perhaps we restrict the blessing by our attachment to the goods that we have, and this greatly limits our ability to receive blessing from God. A bit like a person who does not want to change the job that they have done for ten years for a better position, with better salary, better hours, holidays, pension, etc. They want to stay in their current role for no other reason than they are 'attached' to it. This can be the way we are with God. We become attached to goods which restrict our ability to receive blessing from God. He wants to liberate us from such attachment by requesting we give him the sacred portion which brings us into a place of freedom and God can pour out the blessings into both our material and spiritual lives.

The tithe belongs to God, but it benefits us by giving it over to for 'Kingdom' use.

The test

The concept of retaining a tithe for our own purposes (which the majority of catholics obviously do), means that we are essentially 'robbing' God. The scriptures make it clear that the tithe belongs to God, not us, and that he will bless us when we bring the tithe in. We need courage to give God his 10% so that we can be recipients of the great blessings that he wants to flood our lives with.

Only twice in the Bible does God invite us to test him. The first time is Isaiah 7:10-12 when God invites King Ahaz to ask for a sign, but King Ahaz refuses saying; 'I will not put God to the test'. It is a bit ironic because the King has spent his life putting God to the test and reaping the consequences! In Malachi 3 God is inviting us to test him in respect of the tithe. If the full tithe is brought into the storehouse then the heavenly floodgates will open up and there will not be room for the ensuing blessings.

God invites the Israelites to bring into the temple treasury a tithe of the farming produce (wheat, barley, etc) so that there will be food in the storehouse; the priests and any poor people will then have food. The other consequence of this is worth noting; God's blessing is that the land will benefit from an *overflowing blessing*. This blessing will manifest itself as a *rebuke of the locust*. The farmer will no longer have to protect his crops because God's hand will rest upon them for protection. Strictly speaking, the bringing in of the tithe consecrates the rest of the harvest so that God will protect it. This is the concept of the 'first fruits', 'first born', 'firstling', etc. If the first of the batch is consecrated (made holy), then the rest of the batch will also be consecrated. The ultimate blessing will be an abundant harvest. Indeed, the promise of Jubilee confirms this thinking:

'Should you ask, what shall we eat in the seventh year, if we may not sow or gather in our crop? I will order my blessing for you in the sixth year, so that it will yield a crop for three years. When you sow in the eighth year, you will be eating from the old crop; until the ninth year, when its produce comes in, you shall eat the old.'

Leviticus 25:20-22.

By trusting in God's provision at the time of 'Jubilee' the Israelites will have three years worth of crop from one harvest. They will rest in the seventh year, eating from the sixth year's harvest. They will sow in year eight whilst still eating year six harvest. In year nine, when they get in the harvest of the year eight sowing they will still be eating year six harvest. This is the fruit of trust in God's provision.

Your children

So far, I have focussed exclusively on the literal historical interpretation of the scriptures regarding Malachi 3. However, there is always a spiritual interpretation.

Our primary harvest is always our children. For some of us this means spiritual children. For others it is literal offspring. The Church tells us that parents are the primary educators of their children in the faith. This does not just mean that parents are meant to teach cold, hard, catechesis to their children (good catechesis will be anything but 'cold and hard'), but that parents will demonstrate faith as it is *lived*. Our children will learn by how we live our lived faith. In fact, if our faith is not lived then no matter how loud we proclaim the Gospel to them, they will probably reject it because they will see through the hypocrisy.

Holding onto the idea that the primary harvest for a parent is their children, God wants to protect this harvest from the locust (the evil one). In order to bless us God invites us to bring in our tithe, our first fruits. It is striking that God will challenge us to bring into the Kingdom something as tainted and material as money in order to place his hand of protection on our offspring! Yet, this is the nature of our faith, that God uses matter in order to bless. He gives us bread, transforms it into flesh by the words and actions of the Catholic Priest, and when we consume it we enter into an intimate communion with His Son provided we have the appropriate dispositions!

The blessing

When watching certain Christian television, or attending certain churches, or even reading certain books on tithing, the blessing is almost always seen as something material. The motive for giving a tithe is based on the material goods or services that we will get back from God. In other words, if I tithe, I will get the promotion, the new car, the new house, the better job. Christ did not shed his blood in order for us to receive material wealth! God was able to give Abraham wealth over 1,000 years before the incarnation. God was able to give Solomon great treasures of the world many years before The Son suffered on the cross.

The purpose of Christ's redeeming death was to open the floodgates of blessing upon humanity so that we could once again enjoy everlasting communion with the Trinity. This is the great blessing Christ has won for us. As this is invisible then it is sometimes very difficult for us to perceive it, especially if we are giving a tenth of our hard-earned cash to the Church. This is something that merits much pondering.

We have a very clear mandate from the Lord Jesus Christ:

'But seek first His kingdom and His righteousness, and all these things will be added to you.'

Malachi 6:33

The Kingdom of God, and His righteousness, are a very specific blessing God wants us to seek. That which we may consider important are called 'these things'; food, drink, clothing, material wealth, are all relegated to the realm of 'things'. They are unimportant to God, so unimportant that when Jesus is approached by the rich, young man who wants to 'enter into life', Jesus responds:

'If you wish to be complete, go and sell your possessions and give to the poor, and you will have treasure in heaven; and come, follow Me.'

Matthew 19:21

The Greek word for complete is *teleios* which is connected to the word proclaimed by Christ on the cross, *'it is finished (teleo)'*. The giving away of possessions in order to possess the kingdom is intrinsically linked to our salvation, and the Church has a rich history of Saints who gave away possessions to the poor and for whom the floodgates of heaven overflowed with grace and mercy. This is the manifestation of the Kingdom of God.

How many people who have wealth are we aware of through the media. Pop stars, celebrities, leaders of industry, sports stars, models, lottery winners. They all have possibly two things in common: money and misery. It is truly astonishing how many celebrities have alcohol, drug and relationship problems, sometimes having gone through multiple marriages and divorces. They lack peace and grace.

On the other hand, the Saints provide us with a testimony that is fully alive, the manifestation of God's Kingdom. This manifestation is of an overflowing peace, joy, love, and faithfulness. The Saints rarely had much in the way of material goods, but they had great heavenly wealth (peace, grace, joy, love, etc) which they had in great abundance and which they gave away all of the time. They gave God. This is the kingdom God wants us to have. He wants to take from us all of our miseries, our sins, our anxieties, worries, anguish and fears, and replace them with overflowing peace, grace, holiness and joy. Not that we won't have our sorrows and our sufferings, because Christ saves multitudes of souls through the sufferings of the saints, but the disposition of our hearts can be changed dramatically so that those same sufferings that can make us miserable, can also bring us great joy. This is the authentically converted soul of the gospel who has truly embraced and fully lives Kingdom life.

Seek first God's Kingdom, and all these other things will be granted to you because you will no longer need, want, or desire them!

* * * * *

#5 Armenio, Very Rev. *The History of the Church, The Didache Series,* Midwest theological Forum, Woodridge, Illinois. 2005. P.483.

#6 At the time of writing the nation of England is preparing for the rededication of our land as the Dowry of Mary. This means that we are offering England and ourselves to Mary, the Mother of God, as her special inheritance. This rededication was and is scheduled for March 29th 2019. One could say that we are offering Mary the nation as a gift, an offering, a tithe, in order to break the curse of the reformation and open the floodgates of Heaven.

7. Praying for poverty

'None of you can be My disciple who does not give up all his own possessions.'

Luke 14:33

In December 2017, in order to prepare for both Christmas and the new year, I received permission from my spiritual director to do the Ignatian 30-day retreat at home. I found it very tough, but in the second week I meditated on a very powerful concept which really challenged me, but also brought me much light:

'A meditation on the two standards'

Christ calls and wants all beneath his standard, and Lucifer,

on the other hand, wants all beneath his.

The standard of Satan.

The demons tempt men to covet riches

(as Satan himself is accustomed to do in most cases)

that they may the more easily attain the empty honours of this world,

and then come to overweening pride.

The first step, then, will be riches,

the second honour,

the third pride.

From these three steps the evil one leads to all other vices.

The standard of Christ

Consider the address which Christ our Lord makes to all his

servants and friends whom he sends on this enterprise,

recommending to them to seek to help all,

first by attracting to them to the highest spiritual poverty,

and should it please the Divine Majesty,

and should he deign to choose them for it, even to actual poverty.

Secondly, they should lead them to a desire for insults and contempt,

for from these springs humility.

Hence, these will be three steps:

the first, poverty as opposed to riches;

the second, insults or contempt as opposed to the honour of this
world;

the third, humility as opposed to pride.

From these three steps let them lead all men to all other virtues.

Note that in the standard of Satan, the devils do not grant us riches, they merely tempt us to 'covet' riches. The fact that we *desire* worldly wealth is sufficient to draw us away from the kingdom of God. The opposite is reflected in the standard of Christ where we are to *desire* insults and contempt, and an attractiveness to poverty, but not necessarily to be poor. It is all to do with the desire of the heart.

'Delight yourself in the LORD; And He will give you the desires of your heart.'

Psalm 37:4

Note that the psalmist encourages us to *delight* in the Lord, and then we get the *desires* of our heart. When we delight in money, food, clothing, property, etc, we do not receive these from God. Our heart was created to be the dwelling place of God, so when we put anything else on a throne in our hearts there is nothing but corruption. When God is seated in our hearts, we possess everything because we gain the possession of God. When we have God, we have everything, because we find that in God we have everything that we were created for. Saint John of the Cross in chapter 2 of the *Ascent of Mount Carmel* writes; 'Individuals must deprive themselves of their appetites for worldly possessions, in order to journey towards union with God.'

The Rich Young Man – Christ reveals the desires of His Heart.

Matthew 19:16-22 gives us the story of a rich, young man who desires to 'enter into life', and how Jesus responds to this young man. After a bit of discussion Jesus issues a challenge to him:

'Go, sell what you possess and give to the poor; and you will have treasure in heaven; and come, follow me.'

The story of the rich, young man is a bit like the story of Abba Lot and Abba Joseph as told by the desert fathers:

'Abba Lot went to see Abba Joseph and said to him: "Abba, as far as I can I say my little office,

I fast a little, I pray and meditate, I live in peace and as far as I can, I purify my thoughts. What else can do?" Then the old man stood up and stretched his hands toward heaven. His fingers became like ten lamps of fire and he said to him: "If you will, you can become all flame."[#7]

Fr Erasmo Leiva-Merikakis comments, 'Human nature was, indeed, created by God in order to reach its highest realization in intimate union with the fire of divinity.'[#8] If our focus is on gaining more wealth, more possessions, a bigger house, a better job, why would God grant us access to his infinite spiritual wealth. It cheapens the spiritual life. It demeans the grace of God. If our hearts are set on the things of this world how can we expect to receive anything from God? Yet, God does grant us his treasures even when our hearts are so corrupt that we want the things of this world. He grants us salvation, sanctifying grace, the Holy Spirit, access to the sacraments. He gives us extraordinary treasures. Yet, to gain access to the fullness of his riches requires renunciation. It requires us to renounce the things of this world. It does not mean we have got to get rid of everything; no possessions, no wealth. It does mean that we have to renounce these things and behave as if we did not have them:

'But this I say, brethren, the time has been shortened, so that from now on those who...buy, as though they did not possess; and those who use the world, as though they did not make full use of it; for the form of this world is passing away.'

1 Corinthians 7:30, 31

If we recall the Ignatian spiritual exercise at the start of this chapter, it is coveting the things of this world that is the proverbial thin end of the wedge. This has its own disadvantage to the Body of Christ. If all Christians coveted goods and did not enter into the spirit of Christ's message, many nations would suffer from the fall out of the failure of Christian charity. The Acts of the Apostles tells us:

'And all those who had believed were together and had all things in common; and they began selling their property and possessions and were sharing them with all, as anyone might have need.'

Acts 2:44, 45

The members of the early Church were not being forced to sell their possessions and give the proceeds to the poor. It was a fruit of their having been filled with the Holy Spirit and experiencing a new relationship with Christ. They were liberated from their bondage to worldly goods, and set free to help their fellow man. If God calls us to do similar it is for two reasons: firstly, for our own sake. We cannot possess both the kingdom of this world, and the Kingdom of God:

'Seek first the kingdom of God and its righteousness, and all these other things will be added to you.'

Matthew 6:33

Many of us may think we have taken possession of the kingdom because we have a relationship with Jesus, but if that is our thinking we are failing to realise that there are infinite depths to explore in that same relationship. God is calling us to the heights of holiness and nobody gets there by having any form of attachment to goods. Indeed, any attachments hinder our union with God:

'It does not matter if a bird is tied to the ground by a chain or a thin thread, the result is the same, the bird cannot fly'

St John of the Cross: *The Ascent of Mount Carmel*

I could be wearing a hair shirt, be fasting for 40 days on bread and water, doing several walking pilgrimages a year, having daily communion, weekly confession, but if I have attachments to goods, wealth, job, etc, these penances will have limited benefit to me or anybody else. Ironically, I could be attached to the bread and water, the walking pilgrimages, the hair shirt! Sometimes doing less penance is actually doing more!

Now, there was a second point to the sharing of our possessions, which is slightly more obvious because whenever there is the giving away of goods we may often think firstly of the beneficiary, without realising that we are benefitting as well. The beneficiaries of our goods should be first and foremost the spiritually poor. This poverty-stricken group surround us. All those who have not yet accepted the Lord Jesus Christ and thus do not belong to a Church, they do not have a relationship with God. Such a soul is in abject spiritual poverty regardless as to how their material life is. They are dying! The giving away of our possessions, perhaps to a charity involved in evangelisation, helps these souls. It does this in two ways: Firstly, by enabling the charity (perhaps our local parish) to develop its evangelisation strategy and reach out to such souls. Secondly, the act of penance can obtain the graces of salvation for such lost souls.

The important thing is that we are actively evangelising purely by giving away goods that are perhaps no longer necessary. Eventually, if we persevere, that giving away of goods will lead us to get rid of things that we think are necessary (TV for example), and then we will be making authentic sacrifices. At that point great graces can be given to souls by God, because the floodgates of heaven are truly wide open as a result of our sacrificial giving, and yes, it really does work that way. Why do you think fasting helps in evangelisation, healing and deliverance? Because it is sacrificial, and when we make such sacrifices on behalf of the unconverted, God grants them great graces. We are participating in Christ's sufferings, albeit in a small way.

In an apparent contradiction to all of the above I now quote Proverbs:

'The wealth of the sinner is stored up for the righteous.'

Proverbs 13:22

On face value it appears that everything written above is now going to be contradicted by the book of proverbs, and possibly a dozen other scriptures that will be favoured by the 'prosperity Gospel' preachers. Yet, nothing could be further from the truth. Don't forget, we are talking about the inspired Word of God, the scriptures that are 'God-breathed' (2 Tim 3:16 NIV). Therefore, we must ask the Holy Spirit to help us to read it from God's perspective, knowing that God can grant riches, but he wants us to be praying for the opposite – to desire the opposite. If that is the case what does God regard as 'wealth'? The word 'grace' can be defined as 'God's riches'. The wealth of the sinner can be read as the graces that God wants to grant to the sinner.

At this point I offer my own story as a bit of an example. In my late teens and early twenties I can safely say I was not living a godly life. I was immersed in sin, and very unhappy. My heart was closed to grace and I dread to think of what would have happened if I had died at a young age. Thanks be to God, he got me in my early twenties. I started going back to regular confession, regular communion, led a daily personal prayer life, attended charismatic prayer meetings, and healing services. It was a real turn around, a *metanoia*. So in my early twenties I was closed to the graces God was trying to pour into my life, and in my late twenties I was hungry and thirsty for the graces God wanted to give. I went from poverty stricken to rich!

Yet, how can the wealth (graces) of the sinner be stored up for the righteous? Saint Paul wrote to the Church at Ephesus:

'If indeed you have heard of the stewardship of God's grace which was given to me for you.'

Ephesians 3:22

Saint Paul received graces from God on behalf of the Ephesians, and he was a steward of that grace. His task was to go to Ephesus and allow those graces to pour out from him to them. This happened through both his personal presence and the proclamation of the Gospel:

'Let no unwholesome word proceed from your mouth, but only such a word as is good for edification according to the need of the moment, so that it will give grace to those who hear.'

Ephesians 4:29

Paul proclaims edifying words to the people of Ephesus, and those words impart the grace that Paul is a steward of, to the hearts of those who are willing to accept his Gospel. Thus, the wealth that is stored up in the heart of the righteous man, Paul, can now be distributed to the spiritually poor people of Ephesus. Graces that God has intended them to have since all eternity.

Saint Faustina writes of this in her diary on Divine Mercy, with Jesus saying to her:

> *'Desire to bestow my graces upon souls, but they do not want to accept them. You at least come to me as often as possible and take these graces that they do not want to accept. In this way you will console my heart.'*

Divine Mercy Diary entry 367

Jesus has oceans of graces stored up in heaven, that is why a floodgate is needed (Malachi 3:10) in order to hold back the ocean that is trying to force its way to earth. These graces are the true riches of God, because grace is a 'participation in the life of God'.[#9] It is grace that takes us from abject spiritual poverty to the richness of sharing in God's own life, mystical marriage. This is a journey of grace. No earthly wealth, goods, or possessions can get us the slightest part along this journey.

Indeed, giving away such goods will enable us to fly towards mystical marriage! The beautiful contradictions!

In respect of the Divine Mercy, spiritual poverty, salvation, and all that; Jesus teaches Saint Faustina with regards to the Feast of the Divine Mercy (first Sunday after Easter):

'On that day the very depths of my tender mercy are open. I pour out a whole ocean of grace upon those souls who approach the fount of my mercy...on that day all the divine floodgates through which grace flow are opened.'

Diary of Divine Mercy, 699

The key to receiving those graces on Divine Mercy Sunday are to go to confession and receive communion. That is all! Imagine all of the hardships that people go through in order to obtain worldly possessions. People put their lives on the line, they work overtime, weekends ... 100 hours a week. They put themselves into stressful jobs to earn more money. They sell their bodies, give up time with wife and children, work overseas, retrain. Some will even kill other people to earn money. In England many couples will kill an unborn child, many will use contraception so as to avoid having a family in order to earn more money – not to keep from starvation, but just to become richer.

I was listening to a BBC interview on a social media platform. The female presenter was interviewing a female representative of the African pro-life movement. The African lady was talking about how far down the list of priorities contraception falls for African women, who are concerned primarily with survival. (Water, food, shelter, clothing, etc). Contraception is not a factor for them. The BBC presenter then proclaimed something like 'but if you had contraception you could get out of poverty'. The implication being that children cause poverty! This is a tired argument and a false one, certainly for Africans. If anything, western governments have caused poverty in Africa with their unjust trade agreements and their demands whenever financial aid is offered. Then western news agencies have the arrogance to suggest that African poverty is caused by African children and that African women should either avoid such a situation through contraception or abortion. Such insanity! How can children cause poverty? Adults cause poverty through their greed! Then we sin by blaming children!

In order to have the floodgates of paradise opened upon us all we have to do is go to confession and receive communion on the first Sunday after Easter! The riches of God's own life will pour down into our souls, and an ocean of graces will be given to us. There truly is no comparison with anything the world has to offer. If only we had the ears to hear and the eyes to see, and this is where we conclude by going back to the opening scripture:

'So then, none of you can be My disciple who does not give up all his own possessions.'

Luke 14:33

The Greek word for disciple is *'mathete'* and it translates as 'one who listens, a pupil, a student'. The implication is that if we want to be able to listen to Christ, clearly, distinctly, and exclusively, we need to stop laying up earthly treasures, and start giving up possessions. We need to at the very least desire to give up such goods. We cannot be a disciple, a listener to Christ, if we are not going to at the very least listen to some of his most basic sayings. How can we follow him to the cross, if we cannot give up the purchasing of new clothing that we don't really need, or the latest DVD, new shoes, etc. ?

We cannot suffer for Christ if we cannot begin by stopping the purchasing of more goods, and then start to give away some of the many goods that so many of us hoard. We just need to listen to Him, trust in Him, and start doing as he invites us.

'Better is the poor who walks in his integrity,

than he who is crooked though he be rich.'

Proverbs 28:6

* * * * *

#7 Benedict Ward, trans., *The Saying of the Desert Fathers: The Alphabetical Collection* (London: Mowbray, 1975), 103.

#8 Leiva-Merikakis, Erasmo, *Fire of Mercy, Heart of the Word: Volume III* (San Francisco: Ignatius Press, 2012), 145.

#9 Catechism of the Catholic Church, article 1997

8. Firsts

'If the part of the dough offered as first fruits is holy, then the whole batch is holy; and if the root is holy, then the branches also are holy'

Romans 11:16.

A lot of the scriptures are concerned with what we call 'firsts'. This is for good reason which will come to light as the chapter progresses.

In a lot of older Bibles the first words are 'The *first* book of Moses called...' (*emphasis mine*). The narrative then reads, 'In the beginning...' This is where we get the word 'Genesis' from. In chapter four of Genesis, the firstborn son of Adam and Eve, Cain, offers a sacrifice that is not pleasing to God, whereas his brother, Abel, offers a sacrifice to God which is acceptable:

'Cain brought to the LORD an offering of the fruit of the ground...Abel for his part brought of the firstlings of his flock'

Genesis 4:3,4.

The Hebrew word used for 'firstling' is *bekor* which translates as first born. It stems from the word *bakar* which translates as 'to bear new fruit, to constitute as first-born'. It eventually becomes a legal term. Abel's sacrifice is accepted by God because it is a blood sacrifice and is the proverbial first born (*firstling*) of the flock. Abel offers the first fruits, Cain brings 'an offering'. Abel offers a blood sacrifice, Cain offers fruit and vegetables. It does not take much analysis to see whose sacrifice is more wholehearted and is going to be acceptable to God. The study notes in the Didache Bible state, "Abel offered the best of his flock – a sacrifice pleasing to God – while Cain offered merely the ordinary fruits of his harvest – a sacrifice less pleasing to God. Cain's lack of generosity put him in a disposition to sin grievously.

Separation from God usually begins with a lack of generosity expressed in venial sins." Shockingly this may be used to sum up the lives of many Catholics. Our scant offerings may be a reflection of the sinful state of our hearts. A priest was giving a sermon at the Church I attend and he was reflecting on what is the true sign of a faith-filled parish. Was it the long queues for communion? He did not think so, neither do I. I waited in anticipation for his viewpoint and he suggested that if there were long queues for the confessional this is a sign of a people seeking communion with God. Repentance of sins is the first step towards authentic revival. Those who go directly to the communion queue without first repenting of their sins are merely deceiving themselves and will receive very little from God. A soul in a state of unrepented sin cannot receive the grace of union with Jesus, which is the grace that God is communicating through the Eucharist.

God sees the heart and it is there where mercy and judgement begin. God speaks to Cain's heart, but his heart is hardened by his sin and he kills his brother. His descendants who are detailed in Genesis 4:17-24, reflect the condition of his heart, they are worldly and murderous. On the other hand, Abel is still remembered in our Eucharistic prayer 1 of the Roman Canon, "Be pleased to look upon these offerings...and to accept them as once you were pleased to accept the gifts of your servant Abel the just."

Firstborn sons of Genesis 4 to 11.

First born sons are of great importance in the scriptures. The list of firstborn sons of Cain who are sinful are called by St Augustine, 'The city of the world'. Genesis 5 lists the firstborn descendants of Seth. In a sense he takes on the rights of the first born of Adam and Eve because Abel is dead, and Cain is exiled, so Seth inherits the blessing which is reserved for the firstborn son. His descendants are the ones who 'call on the name of the Lord' and are holy. They are later called the 'Sons of

God' (Gen 6:2). Contrast that with Cain's descendants who 'went away from the Lord's presence' (cf. Gen 4:16). Cain's descendants have many worldly achievements attributed to them in Gen 4, and this can be seen as a touch mysterious until you closely examination the descendants of Seth for whom there are two main attributes, longevity and family, both of which are considered a great blessing in God's Word. On the other hand, worldly achievements are neither here nor there!

Melchisedech – a 'type' of Christ

Noah is the firstborn son of Lamech, and he has three sons, Shem, Ham and Ja'peth. This is the first time that three sons are listed together in this way, and it could be taken that perhaps Noah's wife is the first woman in the Word of God to have triplets, with perhaps the first one out being Shem. Shem is a very important figure for several reasons. The Semitic people are named after Shem (Shem – Semitic), and according to the Church Father's Shem is actually Melchisedech.[#10] Indeed, the name Melchisedech is not really a name, but a title. It comes from two Hebrew words, *malchi* and *tsedek*. The former means 'my king' and the latter 'righteousness'. So Melchisedech translates as 'my king of righteousness' which flows from a defining phrase used of many of the firstborn in the Old Testament, they were 'righteous' in the eyes of God.

Abram tithes

'Melchizedek, king of Salem, brought out bread and wine, and being a priest of God Most High, he blessed Abram with these words: 'Blessed be Abram by God Most High, the creator of heaven and earth; And blessed be God Most High, who delivered your foes into your hand.' Then Abram gave him a tenth of everything.'

Genesis 14:18-20.

Melchizedek blesses Abram, the great patriarch, with 'these words' and declares 'Blessed be Abram'. Consequently, Abram gives a tenth of all his possessions to this great king and High Priest. Abram is giving a tenth of his possessions to his ancient ancestor who is also the King of a city that will eventually be the capital of Abram's descendants. Salem is the ancient name of Jerusalem. This is a very important meeting between Shem, who is the last of the pre-flood patriarchs, and Abram who is the first of the post-flood patriarchs. Abram tithes to Melchisedech and receives the blessing from Melchisedech. In the very next chapter Abram is declared as righteous by God (Gen 15:6), his name is changed, and he receives the name 'Abraham'. Remember from our early chapters that the consequence of bringing in the tithe is that the floodgates of heaven are opened up! Abraham offers his tithe to a priest of God Most High (*El-Elyon* in Hebrew) and the following happens in Genesis 15:

• Abram is called righteous by God,

• He is established in the covenant,

• He receives the promise of the descendant,

• He receives the promise of the land.

All because he brought in the tithe to the priest of God Most High. Some may say the two incidents are not connected, but Gen 15 begins with the phrase 'after these things...' In fact, Genesis 15:1 begins with these two Hebrew words, '*achar hadabarim*'. A more literal translation is 'After these words'. The words which it is referring to are the words of tithing in Genesis 14. What follows next is 'the Word of the Lord came to Abram in a vision'. In other words, the preincarnate Jesus (the 'Logos' as the Church Fathers call him), came to Abram in a vision. Following this, God guarantees him a multitude of descendants, establishes a covenant with him, changes his name, (which means he changes his very identity and mission), and gives him the promise of the land of Canaan which he is standing on.

Jacob – God's firstborn

Abraham has two descendants, his firstborn son of Sarah called Isaac. His grandson born of Isaac's wife Rebekah, named Jacob who eventually becomes Israel. It is Jacob who gives us a great understanding of tithing when he says;

'Of all that you give me I will surely give one tenth to you'

Genesis 28:22.

However, Jacob is not actually the firstborn of Isaac, Esau is. There is an interesting story here that is often misinterpreted and warrants reflection at this stage. Jacob and Esau are twins. Esau is born moments ahead of Jacob and is considered the firstborn as a result. Consequently he has right to the inheritance of his father's blessing. However, an incident takes place:

'Once when Jacob was cooking a stew, Esau came in from the field, and he was famished. Esau said to Jacob, "Let me eat some of that red stuff, for I am famished!" (Therefore he was called Edom.) Jacob said, "First sell me your birthright." Esau said, "I am about to die; of what use is a birthright to me?" Jacob said, "Swear to me first." So he swore to him, and sold his birthright to Jacob. Then Jacob gave Esau bread and lentil stew, and he ate and drank, and rose and went his way. Thus Esau despised his birthright.'

Genesis 25:29-34

The birthright is the inheritance from his father of all the rights due to the firstborn son. Esau despises this inheritance (v.34) and sells it for a pot of stew. Later in the narrative, when it comes to claiming the final blessing from Isaac, Jacob rightly claims the birth right which has been sold to him by Esau, though he does it by devious means. It is nonetheless his inheritance.

'He said, "Are you really my son Esau?" He answered, "I am." Then he said, "Bring it to me, that I may eat of my son's game and bless you." So he brought it to him, and he ate; and he brought him wine, and he drank. Then his father Isaac said to him, "Come near and kiss me, my son."

So he came near and kissed him; and he smelled the smell of his garments, and blessed him, and said, "Ah, the smell of my son is like the smell of a field that the LORD has blessed. May God give you of the dew of heaven, and of the fatness of the earth, and plenty of grain and wine. Let peoples serve you, and nations bow down to you. Be lord over your brothers, and may your mother's sons bow down to you. Cursed be everyone who curses you, and blessed be everyone who blesses you!"

Genesis 27:24-29

So, although Jacob is officially the second born son of Isaac, he claims the blessing of the first born because he has obtained the birth right from Esau at the cost of a pot of stew. The blessing of Abraham comes through Jacob whose name is eventually changed to Israel by God himself. Now Israel is not only first born (legally) of Isaac, but also of God:

'Thus, says the LORD: Israel is my firstborn son.'

Exodus 4:22

This poses a question. Why is Israel called the firstborn son of God? The answer rests in the highly important chronological tables found at the start of the book of Genesis. Adam is the firstborn son of God because he is the first man created by God. Upon this first man rests the future of the entire human race. If Adam, the firstborn, remains free from sin, if he stays in communion with God, then the whole human race will also remain in communion with God. We all know the story, but get the principle. 'First' is the important point here. If the first one is sanctified and remains so, then the whole batch is sanctified. Here is Saint Paul's comment again:

'If the part of the dough offered as first fruits is holy, then the whole batch is holy; and if the root is holy, then the branches also are holy'

Romans 11:16.

If the root is holy, then the branches also are holy. Adam sold out his holiness for the fruit of the poisonous tree. As a direct result of this fall the entire human race, in Adam, also fell. This is the doctrine of original sin in its simplest form. After the first man falls into sin, God speaks into the human condition and begins to single out the 'firsts' so that the human race understands the necessity of consecrating the 'first' to him so it remains holy.

From Adam comes Cain who rejects God. Then comes Abel who is murdered by Cain. Then comes Seth who follows God and whose descendants worship and walk in God's presence. From this line comes the proverbial sons of God, previously mentioned. These are the first born 'sons of God'. At the end of this line comes Noah, then Shem, the descendants of Shem to Abraham, Isaac, and then Jacob who claims the title 'firstborn' from his elder brother. By this point in time the title is a legal one. Israel is not just firstborn of Jacob as a legal title, but he traces his title back to the sons of Adam and claims the title 'firstborn son of God' by virtue of his ancestor's faithfulness to God. God calls Israel the firstborn, or more specifically, His firstborn, at the same time as revealing himself as the redeemer of Israel, the one who would set him free from Egypt. Consequently, the concept of firstborn is connected with that of redemption. Indeed, Israel is redeemed from Egypt at the same time of the revelation of the Passover and that of the consecration of the firstborn sons. All in Exodus 11.

Jacob Tithes

This is a book about tithing, so we return to that position. In Genesis 28 the story is told about Jacob who journeys from Beer-Sheba to Haran, which is the opposite journey to that of his grandfather Abraham. He arrives at a place that was called Luz (which translates as *Almond Tree*, but he renames as Bethel which translates as *House of God*. He settles down to sleep and:

He had a dream, and behold, a ladder was set on the earth with its top reaching to heaven; and behold, the angels of God were ascending and descending on it. And behold, the LORD stood above it and said, "I am the LORD, the God of your father Abraham and the God of Isaac; the land on which you lie, I will give it to you and to your descendants

Genesis 28:13, 14.

God speaks much more into Jacob's life, which causes him to make a vow upon waking:

Then Jacob made a vow, saying, "If God will be with me and will keep me on this journey that I take, and will give me food to eat and garments to wear, and I return to my father's house in safety, then the LORD will be my God.

The vow has four elements:

1. Safety on the journey,
2. food,
3. clothing, and finally,
4. shelter (my father's house).

The four basic needs. As a result of God's promise, Jacob makes a promise in return and concludes with:

'This stone, which I have set up as a pillar, will be God's house, and of all that You give me I will surely give a tenth to You.'

This is a very important element of the concept of tithing. Jacob recognises that all is coming to him from God. 'Of all that you give to me'. He will return to God a tenth of all that God is pouring into his life. This is drastically different to how we may view tithing. It is our hard-earned money as a result of our skills, our studies, our work, our sweat. What has God got to do with it?

'Apart from Me you can do nothing.'

John 15:5

Who keeps the earth spinning around the sun? Who causes the sun to rise each day? Who gives us ample food to eat from the fields (and yes, there is always sufficient food for everybody, but some are greedy, and consequently, some starve)? Who clothes us, gives us water to drink, gives us air to breathe? It is all a gift from God. Without him we can do nothing. Yet, he does not want a return of everything, merely our tithe (for starters!). Jacob recognises that God gives him everything based on God's earlier promise to him, and he will return to him a tenth of everything he receives from God's hand. Of course, he is the grandson of Abraham and would follow the good example set by him who tithed to Melchisedech. However, it obviously took an encounter with God in order to provoke this return of goods. This is no different to what we need to do. We need a personal encounter with the living God in order to set us free and start to make sacrificial giving.

I encourage all those readers who have never had a personal encounter with God to take a break from reading this and invite God into their lives for that just that purpose. Pope Benedict XVI based his pontificate around the personal encounter with Christ. Pope Francis has spoken of it on several occasions, and Pope St John Paul II also spoke of it many times. We cannot grow in our relationship with God unless it becomes a very personal, intimate one.

* * * * *

#10 L. Ginzberg, *The Legends of the Jews* (Vol 1); Philadelphia: Jewish Publication Society, 1968. P233-234

9. Seek First the Kingdom of God

'But when you give to the poor, do not let your left hand know what your right hand is doing,

so that your giving will be in secret;

and your Father who sees what is done in secret will reward you.'

Matthew 6:3,4

Jesus did not really have much to say about tithing per se. Indeed, the only specific mention of tithing that Jesus talks about is to have a go at the Pharisees about their poor disposition when giving in their tithe:

'Woe to you, scribes and Pharisees, hypocrites! For you tithe mint and dill and cummin, and have neglected the weightier provisions of the law: justice and mercy and faithfulness; but these are the things you should have done without neglecting the others.'

Matthew 23:23

However, Jesus does come down on the side of tithing, 'these are things you should have done (justice, mercy, etc) without neglecting the other (tithing).' In reality Jesus wants us to go further than a tithe. He wants to see a wholehearted giving, a no-holding back, giving until it hurts. 'Do not let your left hand know what your right hand is doing.' The story is told of an evangelical preacher, and as people started going for their wallets and purses whilst they were taking up the offering he proclaimed: 'do not TIP the Lord'. Consequently, people started emptying their wallets, thus not letting the right hand know what the left hand is doing. In other words, they did not know how much they were putting in.

Have you ever emptied your wallet or purse into the offering at Church? It is an experience I can recommend. It is remarkably liberating giving your last funds to the Lord, emptying the wallet or purse without counting it so you have no real idea as to how much you are giving. This is the key to the reading from Matthew, it is giving without knowing how much, giving beyond the tithe. Fully giving. The first time I did this I found it a very exciting experience, and I have done it many times since. It is a very powerful thing to empty ones wallet in honour of God. It leaves the wallet empty, the heart full. The outpouring of grace that one receives as a result of such abandonment is beyond measure. You should not check how much is in the wallet, just gather up the notes and put them into the offering without paying any attention to how much you had in there. The majority of us will generally have to count the money in our wallets in order to know exactly how much we are holding. It is rare for us to know exactly what we are carrying on us. Therefore, it is a brave, noble, and beneficial thing to just put that money into the offering without checking first. It could also be construed as foolish, however:

'God has chosen the foolish things of the world to shame the wise, and God has chosen the weak things of the world to shame the things which are strong.'

1 Corinthians 1:27

Well, let's face it, anybody who is going to give at least 10% of their hard-earned cash to the Church must be considered foolish in the eyes of the world. People want to spend their money on their own ends, or at least a charity that has a certain emotive appeal (hungry children in Africa, earthquake victims, etc), but to put your money into the Church without really considering how it will be spent, that requires real faith and detachment because we want accountability for what we are giving. o, we must exercise detachment in this matter.

place. We import that food, the Africans go hungry, we put on weight, and go overweight. Then if we cannot eat everything that we have purchased we throw it out. Crazy! We spend millions on charities to feed the people we have just robbed, making ourselves out to be nice people. What a crazy world.

'And who of you by being worried can add a single hour to his life?'

In the New American Bible footnotes it suggests this can be translated as 'who can add a single cubit to his height?' If we refer to the above translation, many people may think they can live a longer life by obsessing over their diet, lifestyle, etc. It is true that if we are a little careful we might not die a supposed early death, but none of us can live beyond the time that God has already established for us, so there is no point in worrying ourselves over how long we have left. When the time allotted by God has come, that is that! On the other hand, consider the alternative translation. Can anybody add a single cubit (18 inches) to their height? Obviously not. Worrying actually diminishes us rather than improving us.

What would be the point of trying to increase our height. Actually, it is probably 'stature' rather than height. The objective would be to look better, to improve our status in the presence of other people. Many people will have dinner parties to impress friends. They will dress to impress. Indeed, centuries ago it was illegal for a poor person to wear the garments associated with the wealthy (serf versus aristocrat). People will buy a certain property to improve their status amongst their friends. They will buy stocks and shares in order to look good. Cars can be a particular item used in a vain attempt to improve a person's status amongst friends, family, and complete strangers. One can walk the streets of virtually any capital city, but particularly in the Western World, noticing how people will drive particular cars, especially sports cars, in order to show themselves off. This is an attempt to 'add a cubit to their height', to increase their status.

Yet Christ is directing us away from how we may be perceived in the eyes of others. He wants us to consider how we look in the presence of God, and this will be analysed at the end of this exegesis on Matthew 6.

Jesus, the excellent teacher that he is, offers us a solution. He calls us into the observation of nature:

'Observe how the lilies of the field grow; they do not toil nor do they spin, yet I say to you that not even Solomon in all his glory clothed himself like one of these.'

Some will translate this as 'observe how the wild flowers grow...' So, how do they grow? They grow in accordance with God's Word. It is God's Word that holds everything together as per Colossians 1:17:

'In him all things are held together'

Therefore, the 'lilies of the field', or the wild flowers, are held together by God's Word. On the other hand, apparently Solomon, in all of his splendour, was not arrayed like one of these. One would have to ask why not? In a sense it is quite obvious. Solomon clothed himself, not just in his apparently beautiful garments, but also in idolatry and sexual immorality. The wild flowers are a gift of divine grace. They grow in accordance with God's Word. It is God's Word which brings the rain, the sun, the wind. It is God's Word which brings forth the nutrients from the soil that enable the flowers to grow.

On the other hand, Solomon turned away from God's Word. He initially asked God for the wisdom in order to govern wisely, and thus his starting point was God's Word. No doubt he would have meditated on the Torah at some point in his life. However, scripture testifies that he left the path of righteousness, his gaze being turned both by the riches he coveted, and also by the women he coveted. I use the word 'coveted' twice in the same sentence as an emphasis of the actual sin rather than the external expression. The externals are riches and women, but these in themselves are not sinful. Women are obviously not sinful, they are made in the image and likeness of God as are men. Riches are merely an object, a means to an end. The sin rests in the human heart, the desire to possess much of both, to covet one's neighbours wife, our neighbour's goods. Covetousness, is the crime here. This is what Solomon was clothed in!

'But if God so clothes the grass of the field, which is alive today, and tomorrow is thrown into the furnace, will He not much more clothe you? You of little faith!'

The key word in this sentence has to be 'faith'. The person of faith is the one who *sees*. Faith enables us to see the glory of God in created things. In this case it is to see that God clothes the grass of the field, which is thrown into the furnace; yet, he also wants to take care of us, we who are destined to spend eternity in His presence rather than being burned up in the furnace. The contrast could not be greater. Jesus wants us to see how important we are in the eyes of God, so important that His Son suffered and died for us. This is so that he can clothe us with His grace.

'Do not worry then, saying, 'What will we eat?' or 'What will we drink?' or 'What will we wear for clothing? For the Gentiles eagerly seek all these things; for your heavenly Father knows that you need all these things. "But seek first His kingdom and His righteousness, and all these things will be added to you. 'So do not worry about tomorrow; for tomorrow will care for itself. Each day has enough trouble of its own.'

Do not worry! Do not worry! This is repeated at the beginning and end. We are being invited existence free of worry and anxiety, To some this may seem incredibly far-fetched, Y yet, the soul who is in a deep union with God, whose heart is set on fire with divine grace, that soul does not worry, nor suffer from fearful anxieties. They are filled with faith and love and are permanently worry-free.

The Church on earth should be the one place where fear, worry, anxieties and stress, do not exist. This is where God is leading us, and this is what we should be. If our hearts were less focussed on worldly achievements and financial gain, but totally focussed on heavenly achievements and heavenly treasures, then the Church would also become like this. We would probably be incredibly poor, but not lacking! Our Churches would also be full. Who would not want to belong to a Church which lives in such spiritual liberty? It is incredibly difficult to evangelise people into a Church which is the same as everything else. If Christians suffer in the same way as everybody else, what is the point? If Christians are self-sacrificial, joy-filled, loving, peaceful people, there is almost no necessity to proclaim the Gospel because the witnesses spread the good news through their witness of life.

Jesus calls us to 'seek first the Kingdom of God and His righteousness'. What is this?

In the Old Testament several men of God were called 'righteous'. Noah, Abraham, Moses, David, and others. They were all known as 'righteous, and it was God who credited this to them. Righteousness is not a moral quality per se. It is a gift from God who freely bestows it. One understanding of the word is to be in 'right standing' with another person. To be able to stand in their presence somewhat as an equal. It means to be able to approach and petition one who may be more powerful, but who is now treating you as an equal. Saint Paul tells us that as Christians we are 'the righteousness of God in Christ Jesus'. We are also invited to be clothed in righteousness, it is seen as a robe. Putting the two together, when we approach God in prayer he does not see us but Christ. This is because whenever we pray to the Father, with the exception of the Our Father prayer, we always pray 'in Jesus name'. Even in the liturgy all prayers end, 'through Christ Our Lord, Amen'.

We approach the Father in Jesus, and in the righteousness of Jesus. This enables us to approach God in 'right standing'. Not counting our sins against us, but recognising that we have been washed in the blood of the lamb. Jesus invites us to stop pursuing the pathetic goods of this world and to seek first both the kingdom and its righteousness. To obtain the goods of this world we have to work hard. To obtain the kingdom and its righteousness we merely have to desire it and they are given. Both are a gift to be received. The goods of this world are attained through much sacrifice, labour, sweat, stress, etc. They are also short-lived. The kingdom of heaven and its righteousness are freely bestowed by God on the soul who merely desires them, and they are eternal gifts. They are renewed daily in us. The righteousness of God is basically the 'stature' of Matthew 6. It is telling us that our status in the eyes of God is as good as it can get. We might see ourselves as the lowest of the low, the greatest of sinners, the worst person we know, but in the eyes of God we are the best. We are the righteousness of God in Christ Jesus. Our status cannot be any greater! God has clothed us – and in Himself!

Christ wants to bestow upon us an eternal kingdom. Caesar thought he had one. Hitler did. Napoleon probably hoped he did, as probably did many emperors, kings, queens, dictators. Christians have an eternal kingdom freely offered to them, yet we still want to be immersed into the filthy mud of this world. How strange we are?

I repeat, Christ wants to bestow an eternal kingdom upon us, and the righteousness of that kingdom. All we have to do is receive it and we are in right relationship with God, plus we have a kingdom. Every one of us is a prince and a princess of an eternal Kingdom.

* * * * *

#11 A simple internet search reveals that approximately 1.9 million tonnes of food is wasted by the food industry each year in the UK alone. Contrast that with the fact that The United Nations Food and Agriculture Organization estimates that about 815 million people of the 7.6 billion people in the world, or one in ten, were suffering from chronic undernourishment in 2016.

10. Mary Treasured these things...

'Mary treasured all these things, pondering them in her heart.'

Luke 2:19

Without a shadow of a doubt the greatest obstacle to our tithing is what we 'treasure' in our hearts. If money is our treasure there is precious little chance that tithing will become a part of our lives, and money will be the god that finally consumes us. It will not get us entry into heaven, as previously stated:

'Jesus said to His disciples, 'Truly I say to you, it is hard for a rich man to enter the kingdom of heaven.' Again I say to you, it is easier for a camel to go through the eye of a needle, than for a rich man to enter the kingdom of God.'

Matthew 19:23, 24

Frankly, these things are worth repeating.

On the other hand, Mary is the model disciple, and thus the one worth imitating. Before we take a look at what Mary is treasuring, let us review the scripture prior to the headline one, the scripture that references the activity of the shepherds. It provides us with a useful contrast:

'When they had seen this, they made known the statement which had been told them about this Child. And all who heard it wondered at the things which were told them by the shepherds.'

Luke 2:17, 18

I think it is worth considering what the shepherds had seen and were talking about. In summary:

- A young lady, probably mid-teens (16)

- A man

- A new born baby, born of the young lady

- All of this took place in a 'stable'. Not necessarily a western-type stable, but a first century Israel equivalent. Not the best place for a baby to be born

- Apparently, the baby that was born to the young lady in the stable is the Messiah and the Saviour of the world.

- The shepherds had also, apparently, seen angels who had told them to go to the above place for the encounter.

The above would be a summary of sorts of what the shepherds were telling, and St Luke tells us that the people 'wondered' at what the shepherds were saying. The word for wonder in Greek is *thaumazo* and it is found when Jesus calms the storm, when he is amazed at the lack of faith of certain people, when the people were amazed at the leper being cured, the lame walking, and the blind seeing. So it is a very positive word, but the circumstances for the wonder are, to a certain degree, unbelievable. Our advantage is hindsight, but if we read the narrative above without the benefit of hindsight, and then consider that the people spreading the story are somewhat outcast (shepherds), then we may have a different reaction. Fortunately, St Luke does tell us, '*they made known the statement....*' Consequently, it seems that Joseph and Mary provided the shepherds with a 'brief' regarding what they were to say about the encounter. The Greek word that Luke uses is '*rhema*', which is the same word used by Jesus Himself when he is battling the devil:

'Man shall not live on bread alone, but on every word (rhema) that comes from the mouth of God'

Matthew 4:4

Here we have a beautiful parallel. Jesus speaks about the Word that comes forth from the mouth of God, whereas the shepherds speak of the Word that comes forth from the womb of Mary! It is the same Word, the second person of the Trinity. According to the Church Father, Saint Augustine, God has only spoken one Word and it is summed up in Christ. What is that Word? It is *Jesus*. Mary only brought forth one Word and it is the same, *Jesus*.

Did Mary spread the story? No. She 'treasured' these things. The Greek word is '*syntereo*', and it means to preserve, to keep a thing from perishing, to keep within one's self, to keep in mind lest it be forgotten. Mary does this on another occasion:

'He went down with them and came to Nazareth, and He continued in subjection to them; and His mother treasured all these things in her heart.'

Luke 2:51

However, the word in Greek in this passage is *diatereo*, which does not mean the same as *syntereo*. Obviously there are several words that it can be translated, but it basically means, to keep continually or carefully. One of the root words means, to watch thoroughly, to observe strictly. However, both Greek words share the word *tereo*, which means to 'keep one in the state in which he, or in this case, she, is'. This is very important for Mariology. We fallen creatures ponder God's Word in order for it to transform us, to make partakers of the divine nature, to make us like God, as Adam and Eve were before the Fall. The Word that we ponder and keep has a transformative effect. However, Mary is already morally perfect as she was conceived without original sin, conceived immaculate. Yet, she had to remain without sin. How? By God's grace! One way this happens is because she treasures God's Word in her heart in order that she may 'remain as she is' - *tereo*! In a sense we can state that Mary does not need a transformation to grow in her spiritual life and be without sin, because she is without sin. She ponders the Word in order to stay that way and for a continued growth in the grace that she has received, so she can receive more. By way of clarification, at the beginning of the Gospel of St Luke, Mary is presented to the reader as 'a virgin', but shortly after becomes 'a mother'. This change comes with its own graces. At the end of John's Gospel Mary changes from being Mother of God alone, to Mother of the Church, when Jesus speaks 'Woman, behold your son' (John 19:26). Mary receives yet another new vocation and with that vocation comes the grace needed to fulfil it.

What has this got to do with tithing? My explanation of tithing in this book goes back to our giving consideration to what God has given us. Good stewardship of the riches God grants us boils down to our giving back 10% to the work of God – either His Church, or His ministers. Either way, we keep 90%, we give back 10%. This is a work of faith, recognising that we have not necessarily 'earned' those funds, but that they are ours providentially. God gives us the wisdom, the knowledge, the skills, to earn those funds, and by giving back the sacred portion we are acknowledging God's hand in our life:

'And behold... in the hearts of all who are skillful I have put skill, that they may make all that I have commanded you.'

Exodus 31:6

Of course, we can use our God-given talents for our own self-glorification, many do, but that is robbing God and will end in our own self-destruction via a self-indulgent life. Sadly, it happens to many. How many billionaires are in the world who 'hog' their riches, keeping them to themselves, without using them for the glory of God? How much of that wealth could serve God to bring souls into the kingdom?

On the other hand, we can follow Mary's example, and give ourselves completely to God:

'By her complete adherence to the Father's will, to his Son's redemptive work, and to every prompting of the Holy Spirit, the Virgin Mary is the Church's model of faith and charity.'

Catechism of the Catholic Church, article 967

Mary and Tithing

Did Mary tithe? The New Testament does not specify, but it does tell us other things which mean we can assume that Joseph and Mary did tithe to their creator:

'And when the days for their purification according to the law of Moses were completed, they brought Him up to Jerusalem to present Him to the Lord...and to offer a sacrifice according to what was said in the Law of the Lord, 'A pair of turtledoves or two young pigeons.'

Luke 2:22, 24

And again in Luke 2:39:

'When they had performed everything according to the Law of the Lord.'

When you read the phrase 'Law of the Lord' please consider replacing it with the word 'Torah', which is the Jewish collection of books we traditionally call the 'books of Moses' also known as Genesis, Exodus, Leviticus, Numbers and Deuteronomy.

When Jesus was about twelve His parents took him to Jerusalem specifically because of the Torah:

*'His parents went to Jerusalem every year at the Feast of the Passover. And when He became twelve, they went up there **according to the custom of the Feast;'***

Luke 2:41, 42 (bold emphasis mine)

The Gospel writers make it clear that Joseph and Mary were observant Jews, they fulfilled the precepts of the Law, in spite of the fact that Mary was without sin, as was Jesus, and therefore they did not have to fulfill the Law which was written for sinners! However, in order to minister to fallen humanity, both Jesus and Mary have to fully identify with our fallenness. Indeed, this is one of the keys to holiness; the more a person grows in holiness they more they understand the merciful heart of God, and the more they can identify with the sinner.

By way of a small digression, imagine a prisoner, locked up 24/7, in prison with others who are also locked up 24/7. This is how it has always been for them, so they have fully accepted their situation. In comes a person who has never been in prison. They feel great sorrow for the person who is locked up and want to see them set free. However, because the prisoner has never experienced freedom they don't know what it is! Only the person who has never been in prison knows what true freedom is! This is the position of Jesus and Mary. Not only do they both know what true freedom is, they know how we can get there!

Our problem is that we think the prison is liberation!

Tithing is a sign of freedom. We are never free when we use our financial gains entirely for our own self. We are not free when we have the false perception that our financial benefits are purely from our own hard work and our own talents. True freedom comes when the soul recognise that everything – EVERYTHING is a gift from God. Then we can freely, courageously, and joyfully give back to God a sacred portion – that which belongs to Him.

Mary gave God the sacred portion.

How did Mary give God the sacred portion? When did this happen? We have clear evidence of this in the New Testament. Indeed, Mary is the only one who truly gave back to God the portion that belonged entirely to Him. The key rests in the wedding feast of Cana in John 2 when they have ran out of wine and approach Mary, not Jesus!

'When the wine ran out, the mother of Jesus said to Him, 'They have no wine."

(Before I proceed I just want to make it clear that these are not my original thoughts. I have been taught a lot of what I write through sermons and lectures. I have so many resources on Mary I can't find the exact quote. Thus, I honour those who have passed this down to me, but ask their forgiveness that I cannot quote the original sources.)

Mary obviously tells this to Jesus who responds;

'What has that to do with us, my hour has not yet come'

Mary disagrees and initiates her Son's public ministry with these words:

'Do whatever he tells you'

It is actually nothing less than what she has done herself. She does as the Word tells her. What has this to do with tithing?

By telling the servants to obey Jesus, they then fill up the water jars, Jesus performs the famous miracle, and the guests are satisfied with good wine. The consequence is *'He manifested his glory and his disciples believed in him.'*

What is the glory of Jesus made manifest? In John 12 some Greeks approach Philip asking to see Jesus. When they ask Jesus he responds;

'The hour has come for the Son of Man to be glorified. Truly, truly, unless a grain of wheat falls to the ground and dies, it remains but a single grain. But if it dies it bears much fruit.'

The glorification of Jesus is his death on the cross. This is 'His hour'. Who sends him to the cross? Mary does when she declares at the wedding feast, *'do whatever he tells you.'* Remember, Jesus, responded to Mary, *'My hour has not yet come.'* Mary knows what that hour is, the salvation of mankind which can only be achieved by the precious blood of a spotless lamb, that same lamb which was lost in the Temple in Jerusalem at the feast of Passover some 18 years prior to the wedding feast. She is the mother who sends her Son to the cross, and in doing so she offers the Father the sacred portion, the perfect tithe.

Not only does Mary, with Joseph, offer many sacrifices in accordance with the Torah, she offers the greatest and final sacrifice, the precious blood of her Son Jesus, when she sends him into his public ministry. Bear in mind that the public ministry was the precursor to the cross. The public ministry is the preparation, the cross is the final glorification.

'Thus all the tithe of the land, of the seed of the land or of the fruit of the tree, is the LORD'S; it is holy to the LORD.'

Leviticus 27:30

Mary knows this, she has received Jesus, the seed of God, the grain of wheat, and she offers Him back to the Father when she stands at the foot of the cross with John. However, it does not stop there. What do we have to do with the tithe?

'You shall eat in the presence of the LORD your God, at the place where He chooses to establish His name, the tithe of your grain, your new wine, your oil, and the firstborn of your herd and your flock, so that you may learn to fear the LORD your God always.'

Deuteronomy 14:23

Mary offers Jesus on the cross, but prior to that Jesus himself had given his body, blood, soul and divinity as a eucharistic feast to his disciples. He had given himself as the grain of wheat, as new wine, as the anointing oil, as the firstborn, and he tells his disciples, in His presence, the presence of God, in the place where he had established His name amongst His followers:

'And when He had taken some bread and given thanks, He broke it and gave it to them, saying, 'This is My body which is given for you; do this in remembrance of Me.' And in the same way He took the cup after they had eaten, saying, 'This cup which is poured out for you is the new covenant in My blood.'

Luke 22:19, 20

The covenant requirements of tithing are fulfilled by Mary offering her own Son, by her own sacrifice of giving us the body and blood of her Son, and by us eating the tithe in the eucharistic presence of God where his name is established.

Where is the name of Jesus established? In us. We are called Christians. Very often our very names are from those who have faithfully followed Jesus to the point of being called His Saints. Without realising it, our names are not just written in heaven, but the very souls that we are named after are alive and abiding in Heavenly glory.

* * * * *

11. The Practicalities of Tithing

How do we set out our finances so that we can include tithing, and what counts as our tithe, and where do we pay the tithe? First, there are a number of areas that can count as charitable giving and should form part of our tithe. When I first learnt this it was a huge relief and took a lot of the pressure off.

1. Education. My wife and I home school our children and that introduces unforeseen costs, including educational material. Fortunately, we purchased a lot of our material from Catholic organisations, and a Christian one. All part of the tithe.

1. Retreats. If you ever go on a retreat, and all followers of Christ should do this regularly, count the cost as part of a tithe. The chances are that you are paying into a Catholic/Christian organisation/retreat centre, so it is a charitable cost.
2. Pilgrimage. All pilgrimages should count towards the tithe.
3. Purchasing any resources to enable your growth in faith should count as part of the tithe. You are not being self-indulgent (one hopes), but are looking to strengthen your union with Christ by buying appropriate resources. For example, a new Bible, or a spiritual classic.

Where can we pay the tithe? For many Christians this is a very legalistic area. I have heard it time and time again that we should put our tithe where we are being 'fed'. If the local parish is your place of pasture, then pay it there. If you get more from a particular Church ministry, then pay it there. I can understand this philosophy, but for me tithing needs to be freer. I need to be able to follow the promptings of the Holy Spirit when it comes to where I pay my tithe. Thus, I will give to any of the following:

• Local Catholic parish

• Aid to the Church in Need

• Mary's Meals

• Charismatic Conferences (New Dawn at Walsingham, Youth 2000)

• Sion Community for Evangelisation (does great parish retreats)

• Cor et Lumen Christi (Very powerful lay ministry)

• Homeless people (I love giving spontaneously to people I meet on the street)

• Wherever the Holy Spirit inspires you to give.

What I don't give my tithe to:

• Anything that even hints at being supportive of abortion. Hence, I do not give to anything linked to the BBC (including Children in Need)

• Non-Christian charities. I have no idea where the money is going or to whom

• Anything I don't trust

• Secular organisations, particular U.N. charities.

Final points

I have a friend who saves up his tithe in a 'tithing account' and when he sees a need and feels prompted, he gives to that need.

Should we give from our gross or net income? This is quite easy to answer in reality. We give from our net! This is because in the UK we can gift aid our donations and the charity can claim back the tax we have paid. By doing this we are giving an extra 20% into the charity, which is tax already paid.

Now, I don't do legalism, so my tithe may not be exactly 10%. However, I often will give above and beyond the 10% because I will tithe, then I will pay out small freewill offerings, and then spontaneous donations. In other words, I don't let my left hand know what my right hand is giving. The bottom line, this is your hard-earned money, so it is between you and God how you choose to pay the money out. Consequently, back up your tithing with prayer. Always ask God how much you should give and to whom because God may want you to give to one particular organisation for a specific reason, but if you are not listening you may find you are putting your money into something that doesn't need or want it. When I was running my own charity I would always pray for God to raise up benefactors to support my work. Many people would give having felt inspired to do so.

Happy tithing.

* * * * *

About The Author

Derek is a lifelong Catholic who had a powerful encounter with God in 1990 that changed his life quite dramatically. He was born in 1965, Birmingham, England. He is one of eight siblings, one of whom died at birth (Peter), another was miscarried (John). Derek married Lynn in 1995 and they had six children, two of whom were miscarried and now bathe in the Eternal Light. At the time of writing he is working at the Catholic National Shrine of Our Lady at Walsingham and lives in the village of East Barsham, just a mile from the Shrine.

Derek and his wife love walking the local country lanes, nearly always with their dog. He spends a lot of time reading books on the Gift of Living the Divine Will – a favourite topic. He likes to relax with a few beers, or a glass of wine and a good movie, but his most centered place is his garden poustinia where he spends precious moments in silence and solitude in the presence of God. It may sound predictable, but his favourite person and best friend is definitely his wife Lynn. They have had many ups and downs over the years, and acknowledge that there will be many more in the years to come, but they are grateful that they are still together after all this time ... entirely due to the grace of God.

"With Lynn, I can confide exactly what is going on inside my heart, and she listens. When she has listened, she prays."

* * * * *